IMPROVE

Ken Russell is a London surveyor and Puzzle
Editor of the British *Mensa Magazine*, which is
sent to 43,000 British and overseas members
monthly. World membership of Mensa is
120,000.

Philip Carter is a JP and estimator living in
Yorkshire. He is Puzzle Editor of *Enigmasig*,
which is the monthly newsletter of the Mensa
special interest group.

IMPROVE YOUR IQ

The Mensa UK Puzzle Editors
Ken Russell & Philip Carter

HEADLINE

We are indebted to our wives, both named Barbara, for checking the puzzles, and also to Lynn Moore for typing the manuscript

First published in 1995
by HEADLINE BOOK PUBLISHING

10 9 8 7 6 5 4 3 2 1

ISBN 0 7472 5300 5

Design/illustration/make-up
Roger Walker/Graham Harmer

Printed and bound in Great Britain by
Mackays of Chatham PLC, Chatham, Kent

HEADLINE BOOK PUBLISHING
A division of Hodder Headline PLC
338 Euston Road
London NW1 3BH

CONTENTS

ABOUT MENSA

Mensa is a high intelligence society to which membership is accepted from all persons with an IQ of 148 or more on the Cattell scale of intelligence. It has 43,000 members in Britain and 120,000 members worldwide. An IQ of 148 represents the top 2 per cent of the population. Therefore one person in fifty is capable of passing the entrance exam, which consists of a series of intelligence tests.

Mensa is the Latin word for 'table'. We are a round-table social club, where all members are equal. There are three main aims: social contact amongst intelligent people; research in psychology; and the identification and fostering of intelligence. Members are from all walks of life – clerks, doctors, lawyers, policemen, teachers, artisans, nurses etc.

Enquiries to: Mensa   Mensa International
               Freepost   15 The Ivories
               Wolverhampton   6-8 Northampton Street
               WV2 1BR   London
               England   N1 2HV
                                        England

Publisher's note: All references to Mensa in this book relate to British Mensa Ltd only.

INTRODUCTION

What is intelligence?

Intelligence is the capacity to learn or understand. Every person possesses a single general ability of mind. This general ability varies in amount from person to person, but remains approximately the same throughout life for any individual. It is this ability which enables the individual to deal with real situations and profit intellectually from sensory experience.

In psychology, intelligence is more narrowly defined as the capacity to acquire knowledge and understanding and use it in different novel situations. Under test conditions it is possible to study formally the success of an individual in adapting to a specific situation.

In the formation of Intelligence Tests (IQ Tests), most psychologists treat intelligence as a general ability operating as a common factor in a wide variety of aptitudes.

It does not follow, however, that a person who is good at IQ tests is necessarily capable of excelling at academic tests, regardless of how logical and quick-witted they are. Motivation and dedication is sometimes more important than brain-power. To score highly on an academic test requires the ability to concentrate on a single subject, obtain an understanding of it, and revise solidly in order to memorise facts prior to an examination. Often it is difficult for someone with a high IQ to do this because of an overactive and enquiring mind which cannot direct itself on one subject for very long and forever wishes to diversify. Such a person would have to apply a high level of self-discipline in order to succeed at academic tests, but if able to apply this self-discipline is likely to obtain a very high pass mark.

There are many different types of intelligence which we can describe as genius, and people who have outstanding artistic, creative, sporting or practical prowess can all be highly successful without necessarily having a high registered IQ. It must also be pointed out that having a high IQ does not mean that one has a good memory. A good memory is yet another type of intelligence and could result in high academic success despite a low measured IQ.

Someone with a rare combination of a high IQ, good memory, self-discipline and dedication is likely to be a very high flyer indeed.

What is IQ?

IQ is the abbreviation for Intelligence Quotient. The word quotient means the results of dividing one quantity by another. Intelligence is 'mental ability', 'quickness of mind'. It is generally believed that a person's IQ rating is a hereditary characteristic and barely changes throughout life, tailing off with old age.

When measuring the IQ of a child, the child would attempt an intelligence test which has been standardised, with the average score recorded for each age group. Thus a child of ten years of age who scored the results expected of a child of twelve would have an IQ calculated as follows:

$$\frac{\text{MENTAL AGE}}{\text{CHRONOLOGICAL AGE}} \times 100 = \text{IQ RATING}$$

$$\frac{\text{12 YEARS OLD}}{\text{10 YEARS OLD}} \times 100 = 120 \text{ IQ RATING}$$

This method would not, however, apply to adults, whose assessment would be made according to known percentages of the population, as we shall explain later.

What is an intelligence test?

In contrast to specific proficiencies or aptitudes, intelligence tests (IQ tests) are a standardised examination devised to measure human intelligence as distinct from attainments. A test consists of a series of questions, exercises and/or tasks which have been set to many thousands of examinees and for which, in the case of children, normal scores have been worked out for each year of life the test is designed to cover. Intelligence tests may be individual or group. An individual test is given to one examinee only at a time, and requires a highly qualified examiner. A group test can be given to a considerable number of examinees at a time but does not have the refined accuracy of the individual test.

There are a number of different types of intelligence test, for example Cattell, Stanford-Binet and Wechsler, and each have their own scales of intelligence. The Cattell intelligence test is used by British Mensa in testing applicants for membership and two tests are used, one having a high verbal content and the other being culture-fair, using diagrams only. The Stanford-Binet is heavily weighted with questions involving verbal abilities and is widely used in the United States of America; the Wechsler scales consist of two separate verbal and performance subscales, each with its own IQ.

It is said that to have a mastery of words is to have in one's possession the ability to produce order out of chaos, and that command of vocabulary is a true measure of intelligence. As such vocabulary tests are widely used in intelligence testing. There is, however, a swing now towards diagrammatic tests where logic is important rather than word knowledge. These tests include a large proportion of spatial questions. Advocates of this type of test argue that diagrammatic tests are culture-fair and test raw intelligence without the influence of prior knowledge. They are designed to probe your understanding of space relationships and design, and we have included a high percentage of this type of question in the tests that follow in this book.

IQ testing – a brief history

The earliest known attempt to rank people in terms of intelligence dates back to the Chinese mandarin system, when studying the works of Confucius enabled successful candidates to enter the public service.

In the mid-nineteenth century, psychiatrists used information-loaded tests to assess the intelligence of their clients. Later, psychologists introduced the concept of mental speed when assessing performance. Around 1930, Furneaux demonstrated that a relationship did exist between 'power', meaning the absolute difficulty of a problem, and 'speed', meaning the time a person required to solve it. By increasing the difficulty by 30 per cent you double the time required to solve it, but a 60 per cent increase will lengthen the time fivefold.

In 1905, Alfred Binet and Theodore Simon were commissioned by the French Government to construct tests to ensure that no child could be denied instruction in the Paris school system without formal examination. The two devised a thirty-item scale which included a wide range of different types of problems. The concept of 'Intelligence Quotient' was unknown until 1916, when Stanford University translated the Binet test into English and the American psychologist Lewis Terman produced the first Stanford Revision of the Binet-Simon scale. The concept of the ratio of the mental age to chronological age, multiplied by 100, was added. From this developed the modern concept of adult IQ. Mental age remains constant in development to about the age of thirteen, after which it is shown to slow up, and beyond the age of eighteen little or no improvement is found. Adults, therefore, had to be judged on an IQ test whose average score was 100, and their results graded above and below this norm according to known scores. The Stanford-Binet test was further revised in 1937 and 1960, and today remains one of the most widely used intelligence tests.

The distribution of IQ to the population takes the form of a fairly regular bell-curve. On the Cattell scale of intelligence used by British Mensa half the population would have an IQ of between 90 and 110 (half of them above 100 and half below), 25% score above 110% and 25% below 90. Above this central group about 14.5% of the population would have IQs of 110–120; 7% would have IQs of 120–130; and 3.5% would have IQs of 130 or above. Below the central group we find 14.5% having IQs between 80 and 90; 7% between 70 and 80; and the remaining 3.5% below 70. An IQ level of 148 puts the individual in the top 2% of the population and is the qualifying score for membership of Mensa.

The procedure for applying for membership of Mensa is that after contacting one of the addresses displayed at the beginning of the book, you will be given the opportunity to take a test at home. After this, if the results are sufficiently encouraging, you will be invited to sit in a supervised test at one of the sessions that are held regularly. If your score is within the qualifying level at this supervised test you will be sent an invitation to join the society.

The first IQ testing on a mass scale was carried out by the US army during the First World War. Personality tests, or character tests, were soon to follow, but in the 1920s and 1930s studies began to define more closely the general concept of intelligence. What emerged was a recognition of fluid and crystallised intelligence. Fluid intelligence was measured by reference to spatial items (diagrams, drawings or pegs, for example); crystallised intelligence on the other hand was measured through language and number. Pegs involved the use of putting different shaped objects (squares, triangles etc.) into their correct slots on a board in a set time-limit. We are sure many of you will remember having similar toys as young children.

In the 1960s so-called tests of creative ability became popular and were intended to supplement intelligence testing. Gasalt and Jackson's tests of Divergent Ability, for example, required the subject to name as many uses as possible for a comb (how would Yul Brynner have responded to that one!), a brick (easy for a smash-and-grab merchant), or a piece of string.

Further development in the 1980s saw the widespread use of computers and databases enabling data to be centralised for further access and analysis by psychologists. This decade also saw the development of 'tailored testing theory' by Dr Vern William Urry, allowing the subject to be tested close to his own level.

Uses of IQ tests

In educational settings, intelligence tests are administered to assess individual accomplishments and to improve instruction and curriculum planning. Tests have also become commonplace in industrial and organisational settings, primarily for selection and classification. Selection procedures provide guidelines for accepting or rejecting candidates for jobs. Classification procedures, which are more complex, aim to specify the types of positions for which the individual appears to be best suited. The testing is often supplemented by methods devised expressly to meet the needs of the organisation.

Improve your IQ

It is generally agreed that IQ is hereditary and remains fairly constant throughout life. Is it possible, therefore, to improve one's performance on IQ tests? Some years ago one of the authors of this book successfully applied for membership of the high-IQ society Mensa by improving his IQ rating by six points over twelve months by constant practice on IQ tests. We believe that by practice on different types of IQ tests and by getting your mind attuned to the different types of questions you may encounter, it *is* possible to improve by a few vital percentage points. It is these few percentage points that may prove crucial in increasing your job prospects and mean the difference between success or failure when attending one of the many job interviews which include the taking of an IQ test.

A gymnast will improve his performance and increase his chances of success at whatever level he is competing by means of punishing training schedules and refinement of technique. In the same way, we provide you with the mental gymnastics to give you the opportunity to increase your performances on IQ tests.

IQ tests are set and used on the assumption that those taking the test have no knowledge of the testing method itself and that they know very little about the question methods within these tests. Logically, therefore, it follows that if you learn something about this form of testing and know how to approach the different kinds of question you can improve your performance on the tests themselves. It is this improvement in performance that this book sets out to achieve.

Different types of questions

Whilst there is no substitute for practising on actual tests, it is useful to have prior understanding of the type of questions which may be encountered.

The following are some typical examples of the type of *vocabulary questions* used in IQ tests:

Classification

These are questions where a list of words is given and you have to choose the 'odd one out'.

Example: globe, orb, sphere, sceptre, ball

Answer: Sceptre is the odd one out since the others are all circular objects.

Synonyms

A synonym is a word having the same meaning as another of the same language.

Example One:	Which word in the brackets means the same as the word in capital letters? AVERAGE (poor, mean, public, weak, value)
Answer:	Mean
Example Two:	Which two words are the closest in meaning? walk, run, drive, stroll, fly, sit
Answer:	Walk, stroll

Antonyms

An antonym is a word having the opposite meaning to another of the same language.

Example One:	Which word in the brackets means the opposite of the word in capital letters? CARELESS (exact, heedful, strict, anxious, dutiful)
Answer:	Heedful
Example Two:	Which two words are opposite in meaning? curved, long, big, small, broad, fat
Answer:	Big, small

Analogy

An analogy is a similitude of relations, where it is necessary to reason the answer from a parallel case.

Example:	OASIS is to sand as ISLAND is to (sea, river, water, waves, pond)
Answer:	Water, because an oasis is surrounded by sand and an island is surrounded by water.

Double meanings

These are designed to test your ability to find quickly alternative meanings of words. You are looking for a word having the same meanings as the two definitions provided.

Example: Give account of (. . . . . .) Noise from a gun

Answer: Report

Double words

In this test you are given the first part of a word or phrase and you have to find the second part. The same second part then becomes the first part of a second word or phrase.

Example: Mean(. . . .)Piece

Answer: Time; to make meantime and timepiece.

Anagrams

Example One: Which of these is not a vegetable?
HRCYCOI
CNSIAHP
LCCEARO
SPRIAPN

Answer: LCCEARO is an anagram of CORACLE, which is a boat. The vegetables are CHICORY, SPINACH, PARSNIP.

Example Two: Solve the anagram (one word):
BARE SMILE

Answer: MISERABLE

Code words

Example: Which word goes in the brackets?
            PILOT (LATE) PLACE
            LIMIT (. . . .) SPINE

Answer: MITE. The word in the brackets is formed in
            this way: the first letter is the third letter of the
            left-hand word. The second letter is the third
            letter of the right-hand word. The third letter is
            the fifth letter of the left-hand word, and the
            fourth letter is the fifth letter of the right-hand
            word.

Preceding letters

Example: Find a four-letter word which forms a different
            word with each preceding letter or letters.

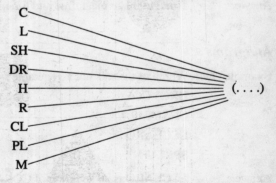

Answer: OVER, to produce cover, lover, shover, drover,
            hover, rover, clover, plover, and mover.

This is, of course, by no means the complete list. There are a
number of unique question types in which it is necessary to apply
logical thought and lateral thinking. The tests that follow contain

several of this type of question which should give you some practice in applying the logical thought processes necessary to solve this type of question in the future.

The following are some typical examples of *non-vocabulary questions* used in IQ tests:

Matrix

Usually an array of nine squares is presented with the bottom right-hand square missing, which you have to choose from a list of options. It is necessary to study the array as a whole or look across each horizontal line and down each vertical line to work out the logical pattern or progression that is occurring.

Example:

Answer: Each row and each column contains a circle, a square and a triangle.
Also, each row and column contains a black, white and shaded figure.

Odd one out

Example: Which of these figures is the odd one out?

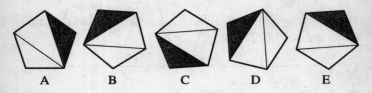

A   B   C   D   E

Answer: B, the other four are all the same figure but are
                 rotated.

Analogy

Example:

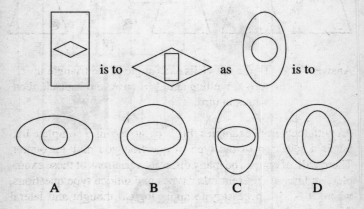

A   B   C   D

Answer: D, the rectangle stays upright but gets smaller. It
                 goes inside the diamond, which gets bigger. So,
                 the ellipse stays upright but gets smaller and
                 goes inside the circle, which gets bigger.

Sequence

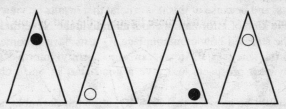

Example: Which of the choices below comes next in the
              above sequence?

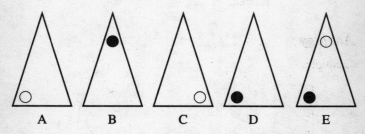

   A   B   C   D   E

Answer: D, the dot visits each angle of the triangle in
              turn, travelling anticlockwise, and is black, then
              white, in turn.

As with the verbal examples this is by no means a complete list,
but is a selection of the type of question you may encounter.
There will, of course, be many different variations of these examples, and many different other types and unique type questions,
where it is also necessary to apply logical thought and lateral
thinking.

How important is IQ?

Cynics will say that the only thing having a high-IQ proves is that
the individual has scored well on an intelligence test. It remains,
however, that an IQ test is the only known and tried method of

measuring intelligence. Some technical weaknesses do exist in all tests, and because of this it is crucial that results be viewed as only one kind of information about an individual. Nevertheless it must be stressed how commonplace IQ tests have become, and that proficiency at IQ tests can significantly improve one's employment prospects and give a good start in one's chosen career.

It should be stressed that high-IQ, although desirable, is not the only key to success. Other characteristics such as ambition, personality, temperament and compassion are also essential.

HOW TO USE THIS BOOK

This book consists of ten separate tests for you to attempt, each of forty questions. The tests are of approximately the same degree of difficulty. Each test has a rating and an approximate IQ rating. There is also an accumulative rating for all ten tests.

A time limit of ninety minutes is allowed for each test. The correct answers are given at the end of each test – award yourself one mark for each correct answer. Some answers will give an explanation, so that you can study the question in detail if you found the wrong answer.

Use the following tables to assess your IQ:

One Test:

SCORE	RATING	APPROX. IQ RATING
36–40	Exceptional	140+
31–35	Excellent	131–140
25–30	Very good	121–130
19–24	Good	111–120
14–18	Average	90–110

Ten tests:

SCORE	RATING	APPROX. IQ RATING
351–400	Exceptional	140+
301–350	Excellent	131–140
241–300	Very good	121–130
181–240	Good	111–120
140–180	Average	90–110

TEST ONE

1. Which is the odd one out?

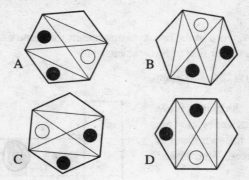

2. Which two words that sound alike, but are spelled differently mean:

   (a) pretence
   (b) dim

3. Which number continues this sequence?

   1, 1.5, 2.5, 4, ?

4. Insert the letters into the blanks to complete two words which mean the same as the words above them.

   BCCEEEGILNORRSUU

   SOMBRE   REPETITION

   – – – U – R – – – –   – – – U – R – – – –

5. What creature should go in the brackets reading downwards so as to convert the letters to the left of the brackets into three-letter words?

AR ( )
ER ( )
BA ( )
AG ( )
AI ( )
BA ( )

6. Place a word in the brackets that means the same as the two words either side of the brackets.

penalty(. . . .)excellent

7. When the plan is folded to form a cube, just one of the following can be produced. Which one?

A

B   C

D   E

8. Underline the two words that are closest in meaning:

   juvenile, urchin, bumpkin, waif, minion, malefactor

9. FORTE is to MÉTIER as

   INGENUITY is to tact, finesse, prowess, aptitude, artifice

10. Solve this nine-letter word anagram:

    GOOD LINER

11. What word in the brackets is opposite in meaning to the
    word in capitals?

    WOODEN (saline, flexible, clear, alert, definite)

12. What word when placed in the brackets completes the first
    word and starts the second word?

    RAM(. . . .)ANT

13.

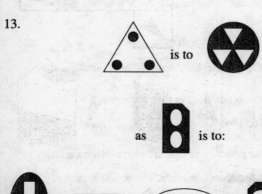

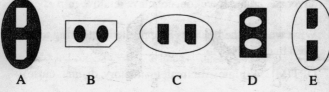

14.

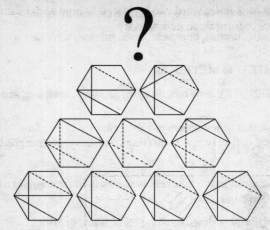

Which hexagon is missing from the top of the pyramid?

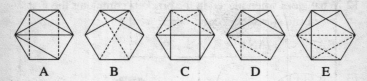

　A　　　　B　　　　C　　　　D　　　　E

15.　HIPPOPHOBIA is to HORSES as:

GALEOPHOBIA is to cats, worms, bees, snakes, sharks

16.　What number comes next in this sequence?

74823, 22446, 13464, ?

17.　Underline the two words that are closest in meaning:

advocate, council, reckon, conclave, endow, mirror

18.　What word in the brackets is opposite in meaning to the word in capitals?

OPTIMUM (glum, minimal, mandatory, distant, close)

19. What four-letter word can be placed behind each of these letters to form three new words?

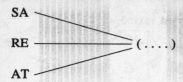

SA
RE —————— (. . . .)
AT

20. Which option below is missing from the bottom right-hand corner?

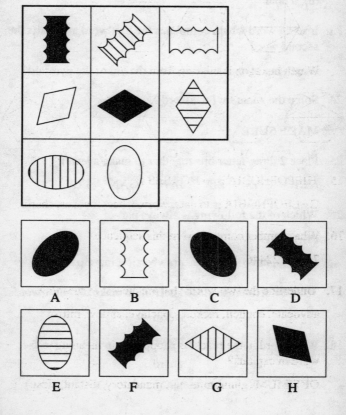

21. Which word means the same as the one in capitals?

    KNOLL

    hillock, knot, skull, knarled, ravine

22. What is a hogshead? Is it:

    (a) a pig
    (b) a bone
    (c) a cask
    (d) a cannon
    (e) a boar

23. Insert a word which completes the first word and starts the second word.

    long(. . . .)gap

24. Solve the anagram (one word)

    MADE SURE

25. Place 2 three-letter bits together to make a jewel.

    NET   CON   ZIR   JEW   GAN   ELY

26. Which of the following is always part of

    PRALINE

    cherries, nuts, liquorice, strawberries, marzipan

27. Which word can be placed in front to make four new words?

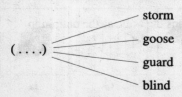

    (. . . .) — storm
             — goose
             — guard
             — blind

28. **Which is the missing tile?**

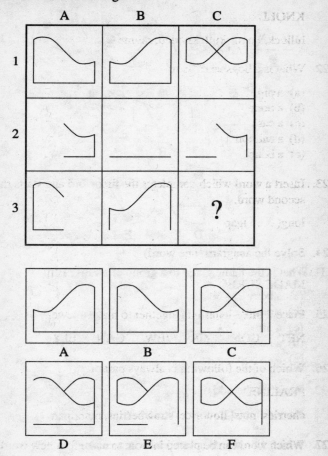

29. Insert the word that means the same as the definition outside the brackets.

    iris (. . . .) droop

30. Which option comes next in this sequence?

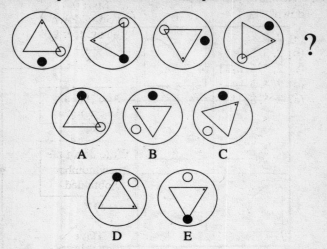

?

31. What is the name given to a group of swans? Is it:

(a) a bevy
(b) a clasp
(c) a dip
(d) a neck
(e) a swoop

32. Which is the odd one out?

clarion, forint, piccolo, ukelele, zither

33. Which two words are opposite in meaning?

serious, ill, idle, capricious, still, thin

34. Which number comes next in this series?

3 – 7 – 16 – 32 – 57 – ?

35. What have you written down?

(a) 2, 5
(b) 2, 3, 5, 8, 11
(c) 2, 3, 5, 8, 11, 14
(d) 2, 3, 5
(e) 2, 5, 8, 11, 14

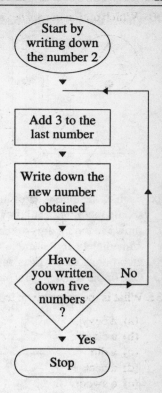

Start by writing down the number 2

Add 3 to the last number

Write down the new number obtained

Have you written down five numbers?   No

Yes

Stop

36. Place 3 two-letter bits together to equal a pet.

PU PD KH OG LA OW

37. Which two words are closest in meaning?

hotchpotch, glacier, ranch, sierra, diadem, farrago

38. Which of the following is not a person?

bucolic, jaconet, ascetic, orator, savant

39. What is the area of the shaded shapes?

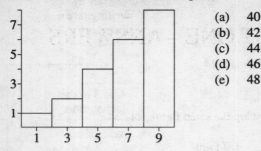

(a) 40
(b) 42
(c) 44
(d) 46
(e) 48

40. Each of the nine squares in the grid marked 1A to 3C, should incorporate all the lines and symbols which are shown in the squares of the same letter and number immediately above and to the left. For example, 2B should incorporate all the lines and symbols that are in 2 and B. One of the squares is incorrect. Which one is it?

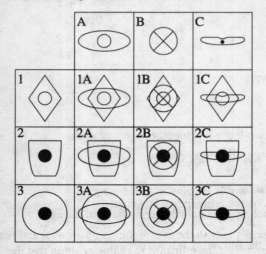

TEST ONE – ANSWERS

1. C. The rest are the same figure rotated.

2. (a) feint   (b) faint

3. 6: add 0.5, then 1, then 1.5, then 2.

4. lugubrious, recurrence

5. CANARY: to form arc, era, ban, aga, air and bay.

6. fine

7. A.

8. urchin, waif

9. artifice

10. gondolier

11. flexible

12. PAGE: to make rampage and pageant.

13. E. The rectangle with the corner missing flips over and two of them go inside the ellipse in the same position that the ellipses had previously been in inside the rectangle. The ellipse remains white and the rectangle remains black.

14. D. The contents of each hexagon are determined by the contents of the two hexagons below it. The contents are merged in the following way. Where just one line appears, either dotted or complete it is carried forward. Where two complete lines appear in the same position they are carried forward but become dotted. Where two dotted lines appear in the same position they are carried forward but become complete.

15. sharks: hippophobia is fear of horses, galeophobia is fear of sharks.

16. 5384   7482 x 3 + 22446   2244 x 6 = 13464
                      1346 x 4 = 5384

17. council, conclave

18. minimal

19. TIRE: to make satire, retire, attire.

20. A. So that in each line across and down there is an upright, diagonal and horizontal figure and a black, striped and white figure. Horizontal lines contain the same figure and vertical lines contain one each of the three different figures.

21. hillock

22. (c) a cask

23. stop

24. measured

25. zircon

26. nuts

27. snow

28. E.
    Col. A + Col. B = Col. C
    Line 1 + Line 2 = Line 3
    But similar parts of symbols disappear.

29. flag

30. A.
    Triangle revolves 90 degrees anticlockwise
    ● revolves 45 degrees anticlockwise
    ○ revolves 90 degrees anticlockwise

31. (a) a bevy

32. forint: a monetary unit, the others are musical instruments.

33. capricious, serious

34. 93 (differences: 2^2, 3^2, 4^2, 5^2, 6^2)

35. (e)
    Write down 2 then
    Write down 5 then
    Write down 8 then
    Write down 11 then
    Write down 14 then stop.

    This is an elementary exercise in computer programming.

36. lapdog

37. hotchpotch, farrago

38. jaconet: a cotton fabric.

39. (b)
$42 = (21 \times 2) = (1 \times 2) + (2 \times 2) + (4 \times 2) + (6 \times 2) + (8 \times 2)$

40. 1C

TEST TWO

1.

Which option below continues the above sequence?

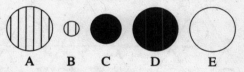

    A   B   C   D   E

2. Consider the following list of words:

KNOT, COSY, FORT, HINT, BEST

Now choose just one of the following words which you think has something in common with them:

NAVY, DIRT, PART, TALK, TRAP, PITY

3. A number of antonyms of the keyword are shown. Take one letter from each of the antonyms to find a further antonym of the keyword. The letters appear in the correct order.

Keyword: FRANK

Antonyms: INDIRECT, UNDERHAND, ARTFUL, SHIFTY, RETICENT, SHY

4. Which is the odd one out?

cornea, pupil, lobe, iris, lens

5. What number comes next in this sequence?

123, 117, 108, 99, ?

6. Solve this nine-letter word anagram:

CHANT PERM

7.

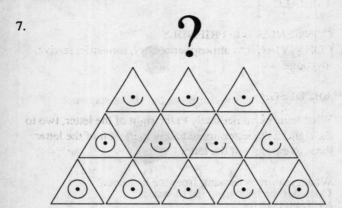

Which three triangles are missing from the top of the pyramid?

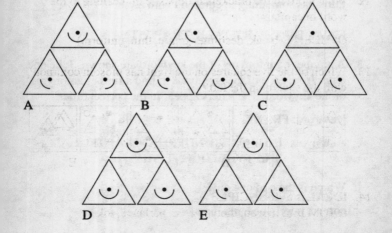

8. Which one of these is not a colour shade?

   TROPCIA
   SMORBEA
   MEARNIC
   SCRNOIM
   TSERALC

9. CONGENIAL is to FRIENDLY as
   CONVIVIAL is to atmospheric, cosy, romantic, festive,
   mystique

10. ABCDEFGH

    What letter is immediately to the right of the letter, two to
    the right of the letter immediately to the left of the letter
    three to the right of the letter C?

11. What creature is missing from the brackets?

    NUT(PIG)SKIN
    TROT(?)HOLE

12. What word in the brackets is opposite in meaning to the
    word in capitals?

    OPULENT (bleak, destitute, gentle, thin, uniform)

13. Which of the five squares on the right has most in common
    with the square on the left?

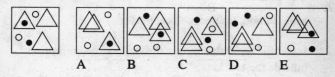

    A   B   C   D   E

14. IDEAL is to PRINCIPLE as
    IDIOM is to moron, diety, torpor, parlance, token

15. What word in the brackets means the same as the word in capitals?

    ABORIGINAL (basic, Australian, primeval, opposite, nomadic)

16. Which is the odd one out?

    dors-, fore-, noto-, retro-, ana-

17. What word is missing from the brackets?

    OWL (LEAD) INVADE
    RAG (. . . .) BEWARE

18. What number should replace the question mark?

36		23	17		14	58		46
	3			2			?	
47		28	26		11	98		45

19. Which of the following is not a weapon?

    blunderbuss, bastinado, stiletto, knobkerrie, hector

20. Which of the following is always part of

    CURACAO

    milk, lemon, orange, coffee, ginger

21. Insert the word that means the same as the definition outside the brackets.

    desert (. . . . . .) brownish crimson

22.

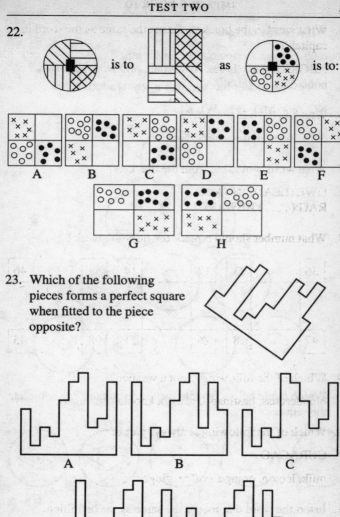

23. Which of the following
pieces forms a perfect square
when fitted to the piece
opposite?

24. Which is the odd one out?

   rabbi, shaman, nuncio, dean, insurgent

25. Place 3 two-letter bits together to equal a loose robe.

   NO GO MO WN WI KI

26.

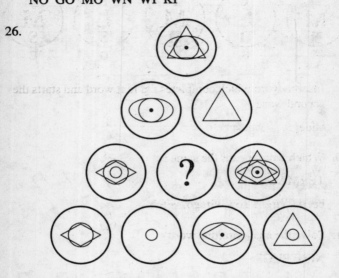

   Which circle below fits into the circle marked ? to complete
   the sequence?

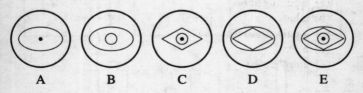

   A   B   C   D   E

27. Which two words are closest in meaning?

   student, convent, statue, carriage, brioche, bun

28.

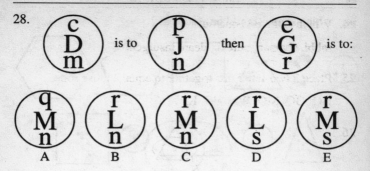

29. Insert a word which completes the first word and starts the second word.

slide(. . . .)book

30. Which word means the same as

TERMAGENT

beetle, virgin, sow, virago, witch

31. Solve the anagram (one word)

NINE PUGS

32. What is a benjamin? Is it:

   (a) a pair of boots
   (b) a hat
   (c) a pair of gloves
   (d) a scarf
   (e) an overcoat

33. Which two words are opposite in meaning?

colossal, freedom, vassalage, delicate, taut, helical

34. Which shape should be placed at ?

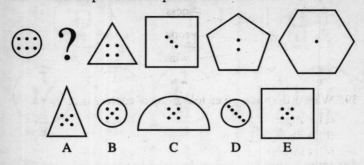

     A   B   C   D   E

35. If the dice is rolled one face to square 2, and so on one face at a time to 3-4-5-6, which number will appear on the top face on square 6?

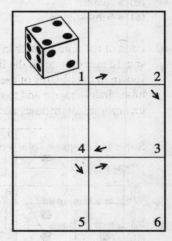

     (a) 1
     (b) 2
     (c) 3
     (d) 4
     (e) 5
     (f) 6

36. Place 2 three-letter bits together to equal a bird.

     ROB   TLE   LIN   DEN   INE   NET

37. Which number comes next in these series?

     5, 6, 8, 4, 12, 1, 17, ?

38. Which word can be placed in front to make four new words?

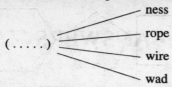

```
            ──── ness
( . . . . . ) ──── rope
            ──── wire
            ──── wad
```

39. What is the name given to a group of eagles? Is it:

  (a) a flight
  (b) a dip
  (c) a swoop
  (d) a stealth
  (e) a convocation

40. Each of the nine squares in the grid marked 1A to 3C, should incorporate all the lines and symbols which are shown in the squares of the same letter and number immediately above and to the left. For example, 2B should incorporate all the lines and symbols that are in 2 and B.

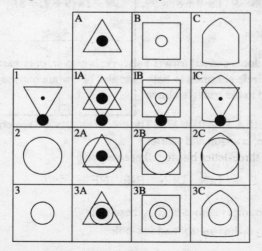

One of the squares is incorrect. Which one is it?

TEST TWO – ANSWERS

1. D. There are three sizes of circles rising from small to large, then descending large to small in turn. The circles are black, white, striped in turn.

2. DIRT: all the words have their letters in alphabetical order.

3. Crafty

4. lobe: it is part of the ear, the rest are parts of the eye.

5. 81: $123 - 6(1+2+3) = 117$, $117 - 9(1+1+7) = 108$
   $108 - 9(1+0+8) = 99$, $99 - 18(9+9) = 81$

6. parchment

7. D. The dot is carried forward always; however, only parts of the circle common to both triangles below are carried forward to the triangle above.

8. SMORBEA = AMBROSE. The colour shades are apricot, carmine, crimson and scarlet.

9. festive

10. H

11. FOX: to make fox-trot and fox-hole.

12. destitute

13. B: it contains three triangles, two black dots and two white dots and one of the black dots is in a triangle.

14. parlance

15. primeval

16. fore- : a prefix meaning before, the others meaning back.

17. GEAR: OWL (LEAD) INVADE
$$\overset{1}{}\ \overset{1234}{(LEAD)}\ \overset{342}{INVADE}$$
RAG (GEAR) BEWARE
$$\underset{1}{RAG}\ \underset{1234}{(GEAR)}\ \underset{342}{BEWARE}$$

18. 4: $47 - 23 = 24$, $36 - 28 = 8$, $24 \div 8 = 3$
    $26 - 14 = 12$, $17 - 11 = 6$, $12 \div 6 = 2$
    $98 - 46 = 52$, $58 - 45 = 13$, $52 \div 13 = 4$

19. hector

20. orange

21. maroon

22. F. The segments in the circle transfer to the square in the middle as follows: top left goes to bottom right, top right goes to bottom left, bottom left goes to top left and bottom right goes to top right.

23. A.

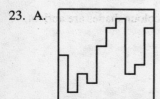

24. insurgent: the others are all officials.

25. kimono

26. E. Each circle is produced by joining together the two circles underneath, but similar symbols disappear.

27. brioche, bun

28. E. Top letter advances 13 letters, middle letter advances 6 letters, lower letter advances 1 letter.

29. rule

30. virago

31. penguins

32. (e) an overcoat

33. freedom, vassalage

34. (c) Each shape is made up of 1 - 2 - 3 - 4 - 5 - 6 lines. Dots are 6 - 5 - 4 - 3 - 2 - 1

35. (e) 5

36. linnet

37. -3
    There are two series:
    5, 8, 12, 17 ($+3$, $+4$, $+5$)
    6, 4, 1, -3 (-2, -3, -4)

38. tight

39. (e) a convocation

40. 1B.

TEST THREE

1. **Which is the odd one out?**

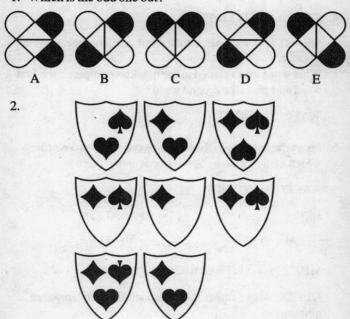

A   B   C   D   E

2.

Which shield is missing from the bottom right-hand corner?

A   B   C   D   E

3. A number of synonyms of the keyword are shown. Take one letter from each of the synonyms to find a further synonym of the keyword. The letters appear in the correct order.

   Keyword: MOTIVATE

   Synonyms: INSPIRE, INSPIRIT, DRIVE, AROUSE, ACTUATE, PERSUADE

4. STAR is to: STELLATE as

   HEART is to: capitate, cordate, cultrate, cruciate, clavate

5. What word when placed in the brackets completes the first word and starts the second word?

   WAY(. . .)ABOUT

6. Insert the letters into the blanks to complete two words which mean the same as the words above them

   AACEGILNNOPRV

   RED   OPERATION

   – – – M – – I – –   – – M – – I – –

7. MULTIPLY is to PRODUCT as

   DIVIDE is to: number, denominator, factorial, quotient, numerator

8. What number should replace the question mark?

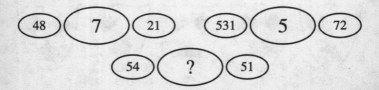

9.

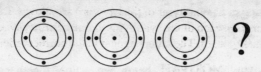

Which option below continues the above sequence?

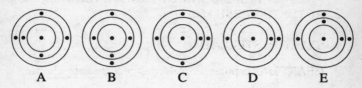

A   B   C   D   E

10. Place a word in the brackets that means the same as the two definitions either side of the brackets.

   promise (. . . . . .) state of distress

11. GROUP CAPTAIN is to COLONEL as

   FLYING OFFICER is to: captain, lieutenant, warrant officer, sergeant, lance corporal

12. What four-letter word can be placed behind each of these letters to form six new words?

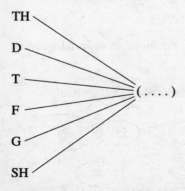

TH

D

T

F

G

SH

(. . . .)

13. Solve this 9-letter word anagram:

    GREY SNOUT

14. Which four of the pieces below can be fitted together to form a perfect square?

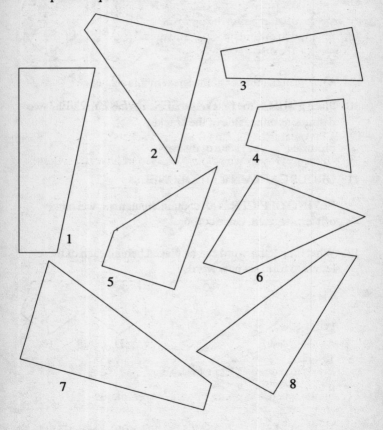

15. SPUR is to RIDGE as

    ESCARPMENT is to: range, slope, peak, rock, pass

16. Underline the two words that are closest in meaning:

halt, abolish, change, expunge, reject, detest

17. Find two words which are antonyms. One word reads either clockwise or anticlockwise round the outer circle and the other reads in the opposite direction in the inner circle. You must provide the missing letters.

18. What written number comes next in this sequence?

ONE, FOUR, EIGHT, THIRTEEN, TWENTY ONE, ?

19. What creature is missing from the brackets?

a light greyish brown colour (. . . .) court favour servilely

20.

   ?

Which option below continues the above sequence?

   A   B   C   D   E

21. Which two words are closest in meaning?

fountain, bed, aquarium, coterie, doves, clique

22. Insert a word which completes the first word and starts the second word.

cave (. . .) kind

23. Which word means the same as

    RUBICUND

    realto, band, golden, florid, sparkling

24. Place 3 two-letter bits together to equal extinguish.

    CH PI EN GA TO QU

25. Which of the following is always part of a

    FIANCHETTO

    pawn, queen, knight, rook, king

26.

    Which option below should logically follow in this
    sequence?

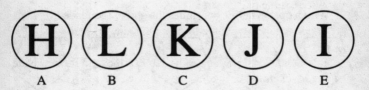

    A   B   C   D   E

27. What comes next in this series?

    $6, -9, 13^{1}/_{2}, -20^{1}/_{4}, ?$

28. Which of these is not a building term?

    gully, vault, atrium, gazebo, batik

29. The letters of the words CONFIDANT have been set out below. Starting at the arrow and moving circle to circle, which must be touching circles, moving upwards and across left to right, in how many ways can you spell out CONFIDANT?

(a) 7
(b) 8
(c) 9
(d) 10
(e) 11

30. Which is the odd one out?

phaeton, landau, pantechnicon, rickshaw, trimaran

31. Insert the word that means the same as the definition outside the brackets.

harbour bar (. . . .) hollow roar

32. What is a marquee? Is it:

(a) a grandee
(b) a count
(c) a mark
(d) a tent
(e) a duke

33. Each line and symbol which appears in the four outer circles, above, is transferred to the centre circle according to these rules:

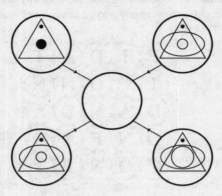

if a line or symbol occurs in the outer circles:

once: it is transferred
twice: it is possibly transferred
3 times: it is transferred
4 times: it is not transferred.

Which of the circles shown below should appear at the centre of the diagram, above?

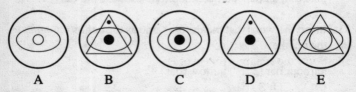

A   B   C   D   E

34. What is the name given to a group of trees? Is it:

(a) a deal
(b) a wedge
(c) a spinney
(d) a mill
(e) a block

35.

On which two targets has 245 been scored?

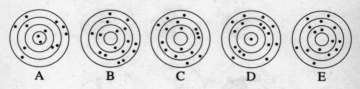

A   B   C   D   E

36. Which two words are opposite in meaning?

wholesome, obfuscate, enlighten, melodramatic,
articulate, brief

37. Which word can be placed in front to make four new words?

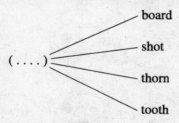

(. . . .)

board

shot

thorn

tooth

38. Solve the anagram (one word).

IRON COPS

39. Place 2 three-letter bits together to equal firepower.

FIR   TER   VOS   INT   SAL   SHO

40.

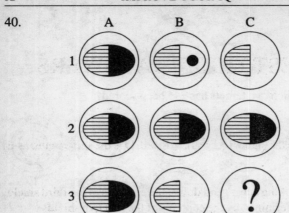

Logically, which option below fits into the blank circle to carry on the pattern?

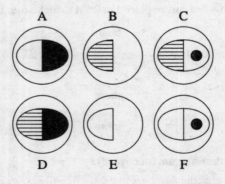

TEST THREE – ANSWERS

1. B. A is the same figure as C rotated. D is the same figure as E rotated.

2. C. Looking across and down, the contents of the third shield are determined by the contents of the first two shields. Where a suit appears just once it is simply carried forward. If, however, it appears twice it is carried forward but is turned through 180 degrees. (Note that when the diamond rotates through 180 degrees it appears the same.)

3. INDUCE

4. cordate: stellate is star-shaped, cordate is heart-shaped.

5. LAY: to make waylay and layabout.

6. vermilion, campaign

7. quotient

8. 3. Reverse the numbers in the small ellipses:
   $84 \div 12 = 7, 135 \div 27 = 5, 45 \div 15 = 3$

9. E. The dots in the outer circle move 90 degrees clockwise each stage, the dots in the middle circle move 90 degrees anticlockwise each stage and the dot in the centre circle always stays in the centre.

10. plight

11. lieutenant: a group captain in the Royal Air Force is
    equivalent to a colonel in the Army. A flying officer in the
    Royal Air Force is equivalent to a lieutenant in the Army.

12. RILL: to make thrill, drill, trill, frill, grill, shrill.

13. youngster

14.

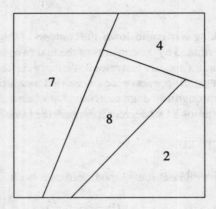

15. slope

16. abolish, expunge

17. escalate, diminish

18. THIRTY. Add the number of letters in the previous spelled
    out number each time. TWENTY ONE has 9 letters,
    therefore 21 + 9 = THIRTY.

19. fawn

20. A. The diamond moves to each corner of the pentagon in turn clockwise. The triangle moves to each side of the pentagon in turn anticlockwise.

21. coterie, clique

22. man

23. florid

24. quench

25. pawn

26. E. LETTER I

    W V U T S **R** Q P O N M L K J **I**

27. $30\,^3/_8$ (multiply by $-1^1/_2$ each time)

28. batik: printed designs on fabric

29. (c) 9

30. trimaran: the rest are all land vehicles.

31. boom

32. (d) a tent

33. C.

34. (c) a spinney

35. A. and E.

36. obfuscate, enlighten

37. buck

38. scorpion

39. salvos

40. B.

   Col. A + Col. B = Col. C
   Line 1 + Line 2 = Line 3

   Only similar parts are carried forward.

TEST FOUR

1.

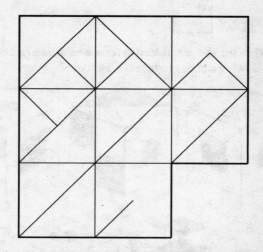

Which option below is missing from the bottom right-hand corner?

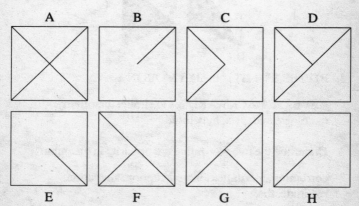

A   B   C   D

E   F   G   H

2.

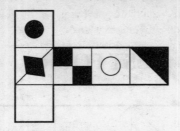

When the above is folded to form a cube, just one of the following can be produced. Which one?

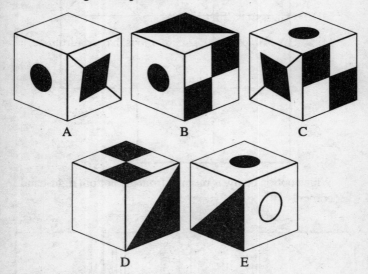

A   B   C

D   E

3. BITTER SWEET is to OXYMORON as

REVERSE BACKWARDS is to simile, metonymy, tautology, syllepsis, hyperbole

4. Underline the two words that are opposite in meaning:

corruption, recrimination, redemption, alienation, rectitude, theft

5. Find two words which are antonyms. One word reads either clockwise or anticlockwise round the outer circle and the other reads in the opposite direction in the inner circle. You must provide the missing letters.

6. Solve this nine-letter word anagram:

   TOURED FIT

7. MINDFUL is to HEEDLESS as

   MISERLY is to prodigal, parsimonious, happy, fortunate, destitute

8.

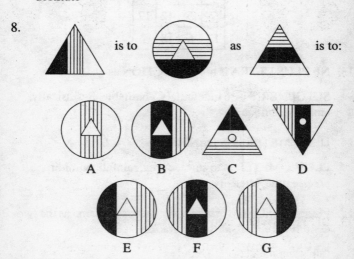

   is to [triangle] as [triangle] is to:

   A   B   C   D

   E   F   G

9. What word is missing from the brackets?

   TIMEOUS (START) PRIMATE
   NURSING (. . . . .) PANDORA

10. Which word in the brackets means the same as the word in capitals?

    FRATERNISE (eschew, distract, swindle, concur, purge)

11. TENDER, DIRECT, RANGE, CREDIT, RENTED

    Which word below is missing from the above list?

    TRAIN, ANGER, DETECT, GREEN, FINAL

12. What number is missing from the bottom right-hand corner?

2	4	6	10
5	1	6	7
7	5	12	17
12	6	18	?

13. NE PLUS ULTRA is to PERFECTION as

    SUI GENERIS is to indefinitely, charitable, intrinsically, amazing, unique

14. DENSIMETER is to DENSITY as

    PLUVIOMETER is to surface area, rainfall, humidity, precise time, intensity

15. Place a word in the brackets that means the same as the two definitions either side of the brackets.

    thin sheet metal (. . . .) repulse

16. Which word in the brackets means the same as the word in capitals?

    GREGARIOUS (reserved, hungry, generous, affable, ferocious)

17.

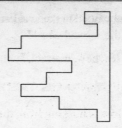

Which of the following pieces forms a perfect square when fitted to the above piece?

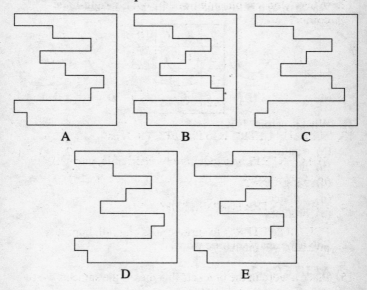

A   B   C

D   E

18. MELLOW, VERGE, EASY, MANNER, JUST, SALUTE

What word below continues the above sequence?

SEAT, URBAN, PLEASE, UPRIGHT, OBSERVE

19. What word when placed in the brackets completes the first word and starts the second word?

    FEAT(. . .)ON

20.

    Which option below continues the above sequence?

    A   B   C   D   E

21. What is patois? Is it?

    (a) a patio
    (b) lies
    (c) gangsters
    (d) a dialect
    (e) brothers

22. Solve the anagram (one word)

    A CUTE CALL

23. Which word can be placed in
    front to make four new words?
                                              string

                                              sprit

                        (. . .)

                                              legged

                                              front

24. Which of these is not a dance?

morris, pavane, ramekin, mazurka, farandole

25. Insert the word that means the same as the definitions outside the brackets.

dashing fellow (. . . . .) leaf of grass

26.

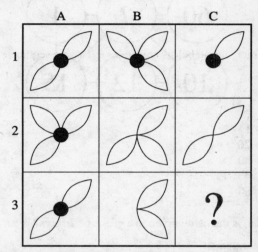

Which of the following is the missing tile?

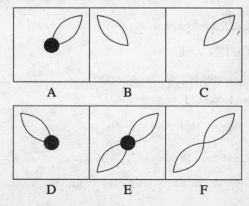

27. Which number should be placed in the centre circle?

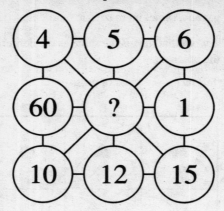

(a) 15
(b) 20
(c) 30
(d) 45
(e) 60

28. What is the name given to a group of arrows? Is it:

(a) a feather
(b) a bunch
(c) a quiver
(d) a point
(e) a bow

29. Which word means the same as

LEXICON

parchment, chair, writing desk, dictionary, diary

30. Which is the odd one out?

mullet, smolt, albatross, gudgeon, grayling

31. Insert a word which completes the first word and starts the second.

fountain(. . .)pal

32. Place 2 three-letter bits together to equal a winter sport.

PIS   SKI   LOM   RUM   SLA   TEN

33.

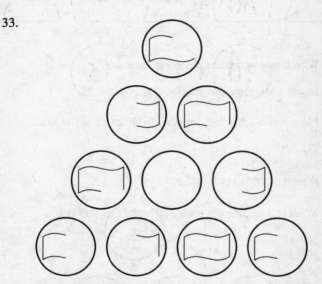

Which of the options below fits into the blank circle above?

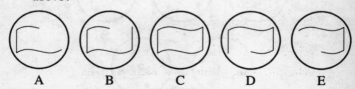

A   B   C   D   E

34. Which two words are opposite in meaning?

obese, noxious, similar, verbose, harmless, generous

35. Logically, which numbers should be inserted to complete the sequence?

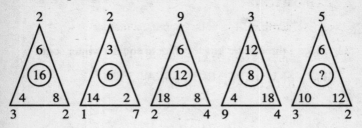

36. Which two words are closest in meaning?

basalt, idol, imbecile, hoiden, tomboy, dwarf

37. Place 3 two-letter bits together to equal a body organ.

TO   SP   CA   EN   PU   LE

38. Which of these is the odd one out?

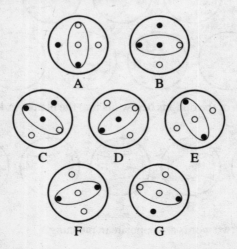

39. Which of the following is always part of

ZABAGLIONE

cheese, sardines, egg yolk, peppers, tomatoes

40. What comes next in these series?

5, 9, 7, 6, 11, 0, 19, ?

TEST FOUR – ANSWERS

1. H. The contents of the third square, looking across and down are determined by the contents of the first two squares. Only lines which appear in both the first two squares are carried forward to the third squares. Lines that only appear once do not appear in the third square.

2. C.

3. tautology

4. corruption, rectitude

5. official, informal

6. fortitude

7. prodigal

8. F. The figure flips 90 degrees left. The triangle turns into a circle and the triangle goes in the centre of the circle.

9. GROAN

   TIMEOUS (START) PRIMATE
   NURSING (GROAN) PANDORA

10. concur

11. ANGER: tender and rented, direct and credit, anger and range are anagram pairs.

12. 24. Looking across and down every third number is the sum of the previous two numbers: 2 + 4 = 6, 4 + 6 = 10 etc.

13. unique

14. rainfall

15. foil

16. affable

17. D.

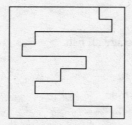

18. URBAN: The first two letters of each word are the same two letters as the planets in order from the sun. Mercury, Venus, Earth, Mars, Jupiter, Saturn, Uranus.

19. HER: to produce feather and heron.

20. B. The outer curve moves 90 degrees clockwise at each stage, the inner curve moves 90 degrees anticlockwise at each stage and the centre curve moves 90 degrees clockwise at each stage.

21. (d) a dialect

22. calculate

23. bow

24. ramekin: a baked dish.

25. blade

26. C. Col. A + Col. B = Col. C
    Line 1 + Line 2 = Line 3
    Only similar parts are carried forward.

27. (e) 60   4 x 15 = 60, 5 x 12 = 60, 6 x 10 = 60, 60 x 1 = 60.

28. (c) a quiver

29. dictionary

30. albatross: the rest are all fish.

31. pen

32. slalom

33. A. Each circle is produced by combining the parts in the
    two circles below, but similar parts disappear.

34. noxious, harmless

35. 24.

$$\frac{6 \times 4 \times 8}{3 \times 2 \times 2} = 16 \qquad \frac{3 \times 14 \times 2}{1 \times 7 \times 2} = 6 \qquad \frac{6 \times 18 \times 8}{2 \times 4 \times 9} = 12$$

$$\frac{12 \times 4 \times 18}{9 \times 4 \times 3} = 8 \qquad \frac{6 \times 10 \times 12}{3 \times 2 \times 5} = 24$$

36. hoiden, tomboy

37. spleen

38. D. A is the same as G, B is the same as C, E is the same as F.

39. egg yolk

40. −12. There are two series:

    5, 7, 11, 19 (+2, +4, +8)
    9, 6, 0, -12 (−3, −6, −12)

TEST FIVE

1.

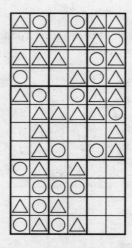

Which option below is missing from the bottom right-hand corner?

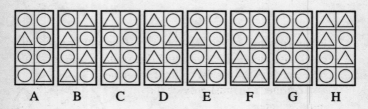

A   B   C   D   E   F   G   H

2.

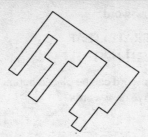

Which of the pieces below forms a perfect square when fitted to the above piece.

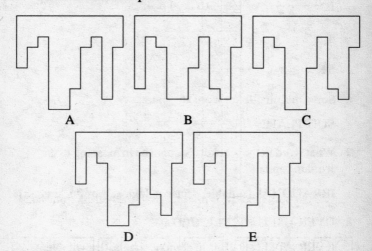

A   B   C

D   E

3. Find two words which are antonyms. One word reads either clockwise or anticlockwise round the outer circle and the other reads in the opposite direction in the inner circle. You must provide the missing letters.

4. Fill in the missing word:

   DOME (MODERATE) TEAR
   NEST (. . . . .) LINE

5. What four-letter word can be placed behind each of these
   letters to form five new words?

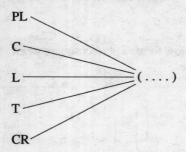

   PL

   C

   L   (. . . .)

   T

   CR

6. Solve this nine-letter word anagram:

   SUIT PLATE

7. What word in the brackets is opposite in meaning to the
   word in capitals?

   IRRATIONAL (suitable, decisive, logical, careful, smooth)

8. OVER-USED is to CLICHÉD as

   OVER-ATTENTIVE is to chintzy, scholastic, irritable,
   imperious, officious

9. Underline the two words that are closest in meaning:

   remove, espouse, erudite, shallow, accurate, knowledgeable

10. What word when placed in the brackets completes the first
    word and starts the second word?

    CAP (. . .) RENT

11.

Which shield below is missing from the bottom right-hand corner?

A   B   C   D   E

12. ABCDEFGH

What letter is two to the left of the letter immediately to the left of the letter four to the right of the letter immediately to the right of the letter C?

13. Which one of these is not a form of transport?

CRTAORT
TROCAHI
ANRVCAA
DRLEEMA
SNOMBUI

14.

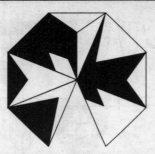

Which section is missing from the above octagon?

A　　　　B　　　　C　　　　D　　　　E

15. What word in the brackets is opposite in meaning to the word in capitals?

SOMBRE (busy, engrossed, funny, garish, composed)

16. Underline the two words that are closest in meaning:

maudlin, worried, sad, slow, angry, tearful

17. HUMANE is to RUTHLESS as

HUMBLE is to obsequious, interesting, facetious, pretentious, deferential

18. Place a word in the brackets that means the same as the two definitions either side of the brackets.

edible bivalve (. . . .) a clutch

19. Underline the two words that are opposite in meaning:

eternal, nonstop, unique, punctuated, noteworthy, lucid

20.

What triangle is missing from the top of the pyramid?

A　　　B　　　C　　　D　　　E

21. Which of the following is always part of

POMANDER

biscuits, eggs, perfume, salt, pepper

22. Which word means the same as

CAPRICE

meaning, dish, fancy, dance, hat

23. Insert a word which completes the first word and starts the second word.

film (. . . .) off

24. Which is the odd one out?

shoveler, whimbrel, paroquet, flamingo, dace

25. Place 3 two-letter bits together to equal a mountain range.

RA   DA   PI   ER   SI   TO

26.

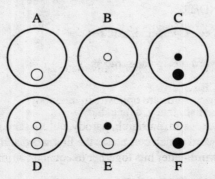

Logically, which of the options below fits into the blank circle to carry on the pattern?

27. Which two words are closest in meaning?

brilliance, escarpment, eclat, meeting, trade, compound

28. Which word can be placed in front to make four new words?

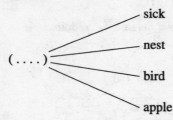

(. . . .)
- sick
- nest
- bird
- apple

29. Solve the anagram (one word)

FORMALIN

30. What is a sepoy? Is it:

(a) a cabbage
(b) a soldier
(c) pasta
(d) a vehicle
(e) a jar

31. Insert the word that means the same as the definition outside the brackets

small sphere (. . . . . .) building material

32. Which two words are opposite in meaning?

glossary, schism, patriarch, parody, union, schematic

33. Place 2 three-letter bits together to equal an animal.

PIG   RIN   GOP   RUN   LAT   HER

34.

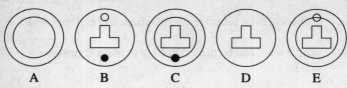

A   B   C   D   E

Which of the options above fits into the middle circle to carry on a logical sequence?

35. Which number comes next in this series?

7, 21, 84, 420, ?

36 What is the name given to a group of scouts? Is it:

(a) a bevy
(b) chattering
(c) dissimilation
(d) service
(e) jamboree

37.

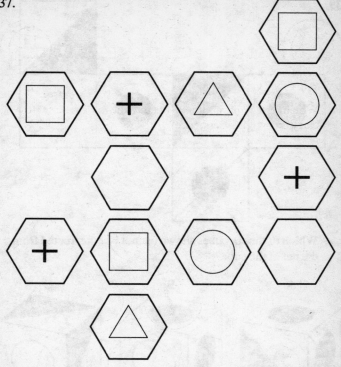

Which two symbols should go into the two blank hexagons?

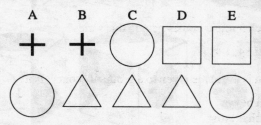

A   B   C   D   E

38. Which of these is not a drink?

tinchel, poteen, anisette, muscatel, grenadine

39.

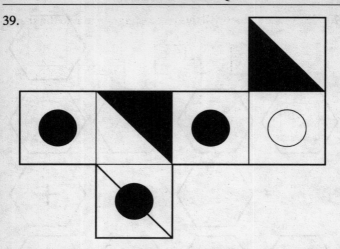

Which of the six cubes shown cannot be constructed from the net of the cube?

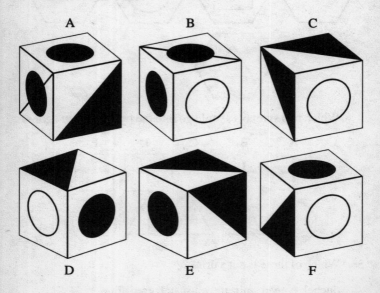

40. How many times will this piece of jigsaw fit into the shape?

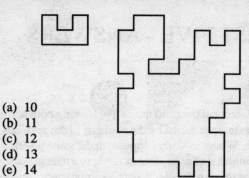

(a) 10
(b) 11
(c) 12
(d) 13
(e) 14

TEST FIVE – ANSWERS

1. G. The contents of the third rectangle, looking both across and down are determined by the contents of the previous two rectangles. Where a symbol appears in the same position in both rectangles it changes from a circle to a triangle or vice-versa in the third rectangle. Where a symbol only appears in a position once it is simply carried forward.

2. D.

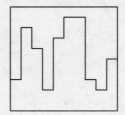

3. graceful, ungainly

4. sentinel: 'nest' is an anagram of 'sent' and 'line' is an anagram of 'inel'.

5. ease: to give please, cease, lease, tease and crease.

6. stipulate

7. logical

8. officious

9. erudite, knowledgeable

10. tor: to give captor and torrent.

11. D. Each horizontal and vertical line contains each of the three crosses; a triangle, circle and square; a black, horizontal striped and vertical striped background; and just one of the crosses black.

12. E

13. DRLEEMA = EMERALD. The forms of transport are: tractor, chariot, caravan and omnibus.

14. A. Opposite segments are mirror images but with black and white reversed.

15. garish

16. maudlin, tearful

17. pretentious

18. clam

19. nonstop, punctuated

20. A. The contents of the second row of triangles is formed by carrying forward parts of the circle common to the two triangles immediately below. The contents of the third row, however, are the uncommon parts of the circles below. The contents of the fourth row revert to common parts and the contents of the top (fifth row) revert to uncommon parts. The central dot is always carried forward.

21. perfume

22. fancy

23. show

24. dace: a fish, the rest are birds.

25. sierra

26. F.   Col. A + Col. B = Col. C
        Line 1 + Line 2 = Line 3
        Similar circles change colour.

27. brilliance, eclat

28. love

29. informal

30. (b) a soldier

31. marble

32. schism, union

33. gopher

34. B. Each circle is produced by combining together the two
    circles below, but similar symbols disappear.

35. 2520 (x3, x4, x5, x6)

36. (e) a jamboree

37. C. Each line of 4 hexagons must contain $\square$, $\triangle$, $\bigcirc$, + in
    any order.

38. tinchel: a circle of hunters.

39. C.

40. (c) 12

TEST SIX

1.

Which option below is missing from the bottom right-hand corner?

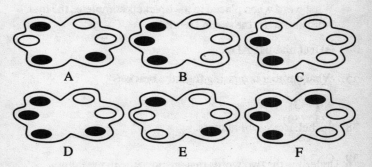

2.

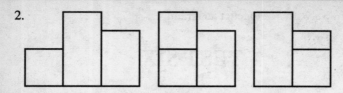

Which option below continues the above sequence?

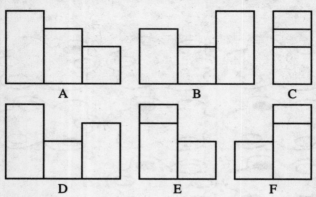

3. Which is the odd one out?

   anorak, mantle, Inverness, camisole, cagoule

4. What word when placed in the brackets completes the first word and starts the second word?

   HUM(. . . .)HEAD

5. What number is missing from the brackets?

   961 (43)
   1852 (59)
   463 (?)

6. Underline the two words that are opposite in meaning:

   angry, cynical, disappointed, gullible, gregarious, caustic

7. Solve this nine-letter anagram:

CREAM TINS

8.

Which option below continues the above sequence?

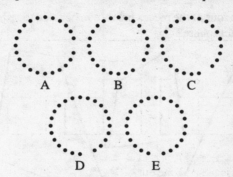

A   B   C

D   E

9. Insert the letters into the blanks to complete two words which mean the same as the words above them.

ABEEGNNT

OBVIOUS   TASTEFUL

–L––A–T   –L––A–T

10. POST- is to LATER as
    MACRO- is to large, last, late, language. small

11. Place a word in the brackets that means the same as the two definitions either side of the brackets.

    a rotatory frame (. . . .) stagger

12. What number is missing from the third pyramid?

13. Which is the odd one out?

lancet, bay, rose, oriel, portal

14. Which four of the pieces below can be fitted together to form a perfect square?

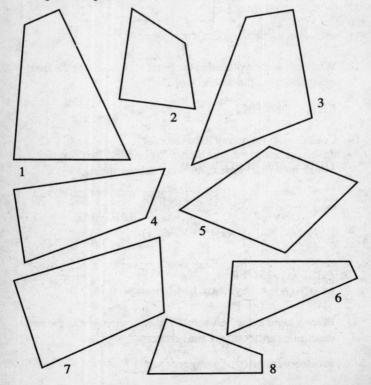

15. What two-letter word is missing from
    the segment with the question mark?

16. What word in the brackets means the same as the word in
    capitals?

    KNAVISH (selfish, fraudulent, narrow, canny, cutting)

17. Which is the odd one out?

    serenade, eulogise, yodel, croon, warble

18. What word when placed in the brackets completes the first
    word and starts the second word?

    KEY(. . .)DOCK

19. Consider the following list of words:

    TIDE, NUTS, REED, WARD

    Now choose just one of the following words which you
    think has most in common with them:

    CALM, STAR, TRAY, EVER, WOOL

20. Complete the words, which are synonymous, clockwise or
    anticlockwise.

21.

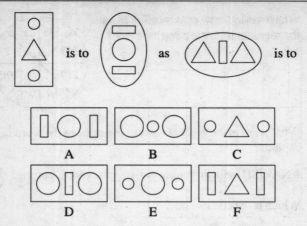

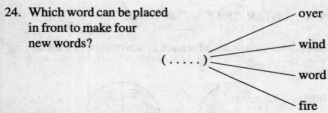

A   B   C

D   E   F

22. Insert a word which completes the first word and starts the second word.

golden(. . . . . . .) gown

23. What is a coulee? Is it:

   (a) a servant
   (b) a ravine
   (c) a boulder
   (d) a waterfall
   (e) a barricade

24. Which word can be placed in front to make four new words?

   (. . . . .)

   over

   wind

   word

   fire

25. Solve the anagram (one word)

   A MAN'S RAG

26. How many squares are there in this figure?

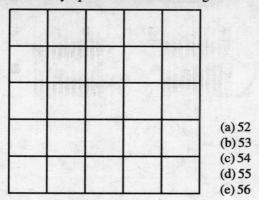

(a) 52
(b) 53
(c) 54
(d) 55
(e) 56

27. Place 3 two-letter bits together to equal claptrap.

GE   BU   LI   HA   UM   NK

28. Which of the following is always part of a

JABOT

cardboard, lace, hessian, steel mesh, porcelain

29. Which word means the same as

CODDLE

sumach, wrap, swaddle, indulge, cook

30. Insert the word that means the same as the definition outside the brackets.

hurl (. . . . . .) boat

31. Which option fits into the blank circle to carry on a logical sequence?

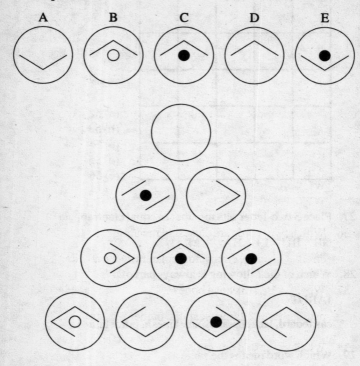

A   B   C   D   E

32. What is the name given to a group of curs? Is it:

   (a) a bark
   (b) a cowardice
   (c) a race
   (d) a stack
   (e) a trail

33. Which two words are opposite in meaning?

   hackneyed, thraldom, generosity, liberty, interface, terror

34. Which one of these cannot have its six letters rearranged into a six-letter word?

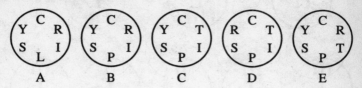

A   B   C   D   E

35. Which of these is not a musical instrument?

LUFET
RAHP
ABUT
WETOR
TOCREN

36. Which two words are closest in meaning?

circular, theatre, circus, funicular, railway, arcade

37. Which of these is not a bone?

patella, carpus, tartar, scapula, humerus

38. Which is the odd one out?

shantung, organdie, yashmak, hessian, chamois

39. What is the value of this angle?

(a) 55°
(b) 60°
(c) 65°
(d) 70°
(e) 75°

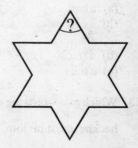

40.

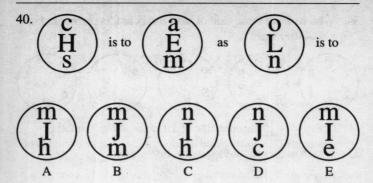

is to ... as ... is to

A   B   C   D   E

TEST SIX – ANSWERS

1. D. Looking along each line and down each column, the contents of the third cloud are determined by the contents of the first two clouds in the following way. Where just one ellipse appears in a certain position it is carried forward to the third cloud. However, where two ellipses appear in the same position they are carried forward, but two white ellipses change to black and vice-versa.

2. A. At the first stage the three parts are in the position illustrated. At each subsequent stage the figure (i) moves to the right one position at a time.

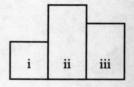

3. camisole: it is an undergarment, the rest are outer garments.

4. DRUM: to produce humdrum and drumhead.

5. 62. Reverse each number and take the square root of the component parts;

$$961 \rightarrow 169 \ \sqrt{16} = 4, \sqrt{9} = 3 = 43$$
Therefore, $463 \rightarrow 364 \ \sqrt{36} = 6, \sqrt{4} = 2 = 62$

6. cynical, gullible

7. MISCREANT

8. B. The gap moves clockwise, first by one dot, then two dots, then three dots etc.

9. blatant, elegant

10. large

11. reel

12. 12: $7 \times 8 \div 4 = 14$, $5 \times 4 \div 2 = 10$, $18 \times 6 \div 9 = 12$

13. portal: it is a type of door, the rest are types of windows.

14.

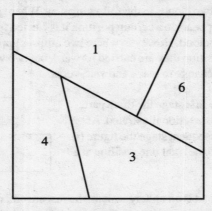

15. AS. Each two-letter word is produced by the numbers in opposite segments. Take the corresponding letters of the alphabet in respect of their numbered position A=1, B=2 etc. For example: 235 = 23, 5 = WE and 119 = 1, 19 = AS. (The letters produced by 11, 9 = KI do not result in a two-letter word.

16. fraudulent

17. eulogise: it is spoken, the rest are sung.

18. PAD, to produce keypad and paddock.

19. STAR: they all produce another word when read backwards.

20. waxworks, effigies

21. B. The large ellipse becomes a rectangle, the small rectangle becomes a small circle, the triangles become large circles.

22. wedding

23. (b) a ravine

24. cross

25. anagrams

26. (d) 55
    (1^2) $1 - 5 \times 5$
    (2^2) $4 - 4 \times 4$
    (3^2) $9 - 3 \times 3$
    (4^2) $16 - 2 \times 2$
    (5^2) $25 - 1 \times 1$

27. bunkum

28. lace

29. indulge

30. launch

31. C. Each circle is produced by combining the two lower circles, but similar symbols disappear.

32. (b) a cowardice

33. thraldom, liberty

34. C. The others are lyrics, crispy, script, crypts.

35. WETOR = TOWER. The others are: flute, harp, tuba, cornet.

36. funicular, railway

37. tartar

38. yashmak: the rest are all names of materials.

39. (b) 60°

40. A.
```
    c       b      a         o      n       m
      H   G   F   E           L   K   J   I
        s r q p o n m           n m l k j i h
```

TEST SEVEN

1.

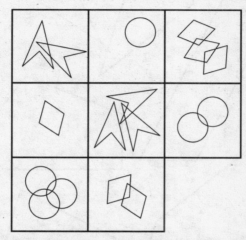

Which option below is missing from the bottom right-hand corner?

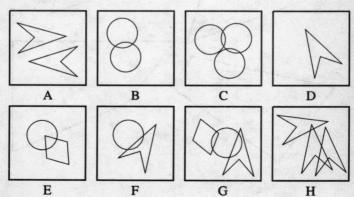

2. Which four of the pieces below can be fitted together to form a perfect square?

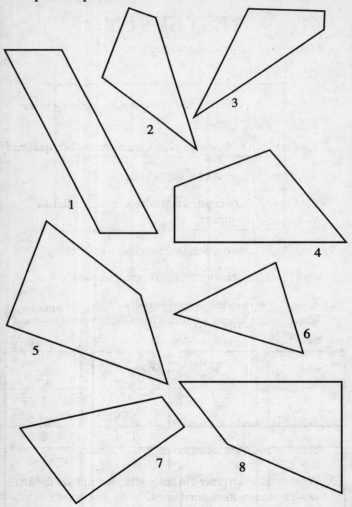

3. Which word in the brackets means the same as the word in capitals?

    PRINCIPLE (majesty, dictum, cost, capital, leader)

4. Solve this nine-letter word anagram:

    DON IN RACE

5. Which word in the brackets is opposite in meaning to the word in capitals?

    ACRIMONIOUS (benign, sharp, churlish, smooth, qualified)

6. WARLOCK is to MALE WITCH as

    SHAMAN is to wizard, witch doctor, sorcerer, female vampire, witch-hunter

7. Underline the two words that are closest in meaning.

    casual, largess, charity, mischief, great, destiny

8. Which of the five boxes on the right has most in common with the box on the left?

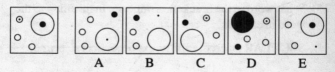

    A   B   C   D   E

9. Which is the odd one out?

    bisque, ebony, jet, sable, raven

10. What word when placed in the brackets completes the first word and starts the second word?

    HAT(. . .)DEN

11. What word is missing from the brackets?

    BARONET (ROBIN) REBUILD

    DREADED (. . . . .) TEMPEST

12. Which word in the brackets means the same as the word in capitals?

    VOLUBLE (optional, articulate, ample, epicurean, avid)

13. Underline the two words that are opposite in meaning:

    flexible, intrepid, patient, afraid, elated, cheap

14.

    Which option below continues the above sequence?

    A   B   C   D   E

15. What word in the brackets is opposite in meaning to the word in capitals?

    SECULAR (sacred, earthly, exposed, liberal, prime)

16. Which two words that sound alike but are spelled differently mean:

    (a) instrument
    (b) kind of fine thin silk

17. 2025 is to 45 as

    6724 is to 43, 54, 82, 136 or 336

18. **A B C D E F G H**

What letter is two to the right of the letter three to the left of the letter two to the right of the letter three to the left of the letter H?

19. Underline the two words that are closest in meaning:

apply, patronise, fuse, gainsay, revenue, contradict

20.

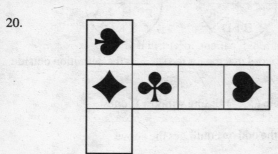

When the above is folded to form a cube, just one of the following can be produced. Which one?

A   B   C

D   E

21. Which of these is not a mineral?

    gneiss, graphite, puncheon, bauxite, antimony

22. Complete the words which are synonyms, clockwise or
    anticlockwise

23. Insert the word that means the same as the definition outside
    the brackets

    turban cloth (. . . .) sliding window frame

24. Which is the odd one out?

    jacinth, chicane, sardonyx, carbuncle, marcasite

25. What is the name given to a group of herons? Is it:

    (a) a span
    (b) a stack
    (c) a skulk
    (d) a string
    (e) a siege

26. Which two words are closest in meaning?

    cafe, wig, umbrella, gaffe, blunder, pontoon

27. Place 3 two-letter bits together to equal a garment

    RO   UD   PR   AL   ES   SH

28.

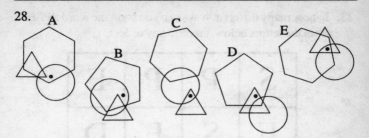

Which of these sets of shapes is most like the example below?

29. Which of the following is always part of?

SUCCOTASH

cabbage, corn, butter, bread, honey

30. What is a scow? Is it:

    (a) a frown
    (b) a crane
    (c) a game
    (d) a bone
    (e) a boat

31. Insert a word which completes the first word and starts the
    second word

    swag(. . .)power

32. Which two words are opposite in meaning?

    vexatious, vivacious, fixation, satisfying, divided, fanciful

33. In how many different ways can you form the word SPEED
   from the letters below, taken in any order?

S	P	P	E
E	S	E	D

   (a) 18
   (b) 20
   (c) 22
   (d) 24
   (e) 26

34. Which word means the same as

   BURLESQUE

   caricature, circus, stage, magical, mime

35.

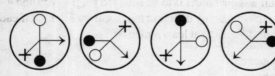

Which option below comes next in this sequence?

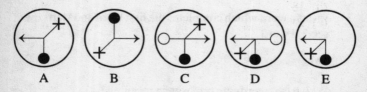

36. Which word can be placed in front to make four new words?

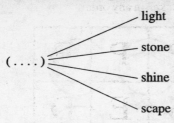

(. . . .) light
stone
shine
scape

37. Which one of these is not a boat?

CHUNLA
FIKSF
ONACE
HCAYT
TOBLET

38. Solve the anagram (one word)

CLUE A GOAT

39. A team of 4 gymnasts is to be selected from 4 men and 4 women. How many different teams can be selected if each team must include at least 3 men?

(a) 15
(b) 16
(c) 17
(d) 18
(e) 19

40. Logically, which option fits into the blank circle to carry on the pattern?

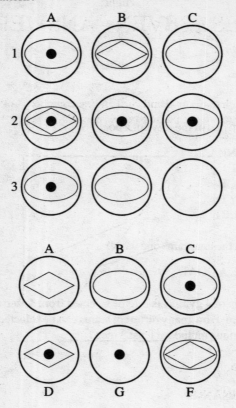

TEST SEVEN – ANSWERS

1. D. Each horizontal and vertical line contains a box with a different symbol, also a box with one symbol, two symbols and three symbols.

2.

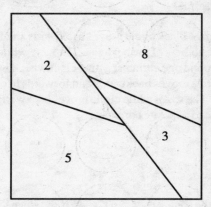

3. dictum

4. ORDINANCE

5. benign

6. witch doctor

7. largess, charity

8. A. It contains a large circle, three small white circles, a small back circle and a dot.

9. bisque: it is white, the rest are black.

10. RED: to produce hatred and redden.

11. TAMED

   BAR[2]O[5]NET ([1]R[2]O[3]B[4]I[5]N) R[1]EB[3]U[4]ILD

   DR[2]EA[5]DED ([1]T[2]A[3]M[4]E[5]D) T[1]EM[3]P[4]EST

12. articulate

13. intrepid, afraid

14. E. The large black circle moves backwards and forwards to opposite corners of the hexagon. The large white circle moves round one corner at a time clockwise. The small black circle moves backwards and forwards to opposite corners. The small white circle moves backwards and forwards to opposite corners.

15. sacred

16. tool, tulle

17. 82. It is the square root of 6724. 45 is the square root of 2025.

18. F

19. gainsay, contradict

20. D.

21. puncheon

22. deserter, absentee

23. sash

24. chicane: the others are all semi-precious jewels.

25. (e) a siege

26. gaffe, blunder

27. shroud

28. E. The dot appears in triangle, circle and hexagon.

29. corn

30. (e) a boat

31. man

32. vexatious, satisfying

33. (d) S2 × P2 × E6 = 24

34. caricature

35. E.

   —● moves 90 degrees clockwise
   —○ moves 135 degrees anticlockwise
   —✗ moves 180 degrees
   —→ moves 45 degrees clockwise

36. moon

37. TOBLET = BOTTLE. The boats are: launch, skiff, canoe and yacht

38. Catalogue

39. (c) 17   (3 men) $\dfrac{4 \times 3 \times 2}{1 \times 2 \times 3} = 4$

             (4 men) $\dfrac{1 \times 2 \times 3 \times 4}{1 \times 2 \times 3 \times 4} = 1$

             (1 woman) $\dfrac{4}{1} = 4$

Total: $4 \times 4 + 1 = 17$

40. B. Col. A + Col. B = Col. C
    Line 1 + Line 2 = Line 3
    Only similar symbols are carried forward

TEST EIGHT

1.

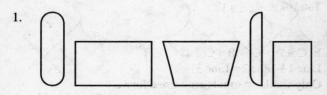

Which option below continues the above sequence?

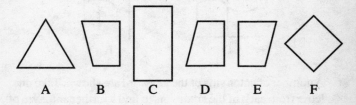

A   B   C   D   E   F

2. What word when placed in the brackets completes the first word and starts the second word?

   TAIL(. . . .)BREAK

3. What word is missing from the brackets?

   STIRRED (RIDER) CREEPER

   SOUPCON (. . . . .) UPRIGHT

4. What word in the brackets means the same as the word in capitals?

   CROOKED (rough, crumpled, ruthless, round, angled)

5.

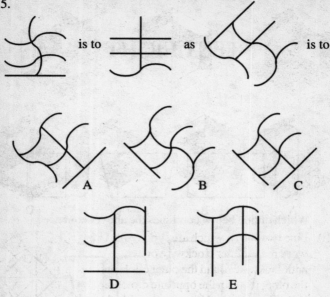

6. A number of antonyms of the keyword are shown. Take one letter from each of the antonyms to find a further antonym of the keyword. The letters appear in the correct order.

Keyword: POLITE

Antonyms: UNCULTURED, IMPERTINENT,
            DISCOURTEOUS, IMPUDENT,
            UNREFINED

7. Solve this nine-letter word anagram:

ONCE A WALL

8. Solve this nine-letter word anagram:

THERE A BIN

9.

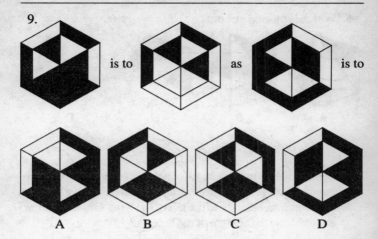

is to ... as ... is to

A   B   C   D

10. Fine two words which are synonyms. One
    word reads either clockwise or
    anticlockwise round the outer circle and
    the other reads in the opposite direction
    in the inner circle. You must provide the
    missing letters.

11. What word in the brackets is opposite in meaning to the
    word in capitals?

    EFFICACIOUS (productive, dull, useless, boring, difficult)

12. Which two words that sound alike but are spelled differently
    mean:

    (a) encroach
    (b) spoke violently

13. STULTIFYING is to STUPEFYING as

    PEDESTRIAN is to painful, ponderous, stereotyped,
    vacuous, parochial

14. Which is the odd one out?

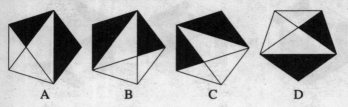

A   B   C   D

15. ABCDEFGH

Which letter is immediately to the right of the letter which is three to the left of the letter which is placed midway between the letter immediately to the left of the letter G and the letter immediately to the right of the letter A?

16. Underline the two words that are closest in meaning:

pacify, mock, chaff, mob, mix, cool

17. Which is the odd one out?

traipse, sprint, perambulate, promenade, toddle

18. What word when placed in the brackets completes the first word and starts the second word?

NOSE(. . . .)WAGON

19. Which one of these is not a fruit?

TMUASAS
GLOATEN
IGABONE
DOOCVAA
KUINMPP

20.

Which option below continues the above sequence?

A   B   C   D

21. Place 3 two-letter bits together to equal a puzzle game

LO   DO   GS   JI   TO   AW

22. Which word can be placed in front to make four new words?

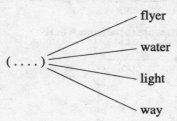

(. . . .) ——— flyer

——— water

——— light

——— way

23. Insert the word that means the same as the definitions outside the brackets.

plunder (. . . .) ancient wine

24. What is taupe? Is it:

(a) a macaw
(b) dope
(c) brownish colour
(d) a pearl
(e) a barn

25. Which is the odd one out?

dromond, sampan, barouche, whaler, caravel

26. Logically, which digit should replace the ⑦ ?

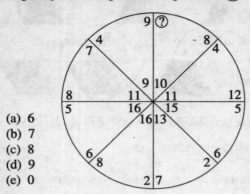

(a) 6
(b) 7
(c) 8
(d) 9
(e) 0

27. How many different routes are there from A to B?

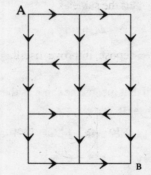

(a) 8
(b) 9
(c) 10
(d) 11
(e) 12

28. Which two words are closest in meaning?

cauldron, restaurant, brasserie, lingerie, barbecue, heliotrope

29. Which of the following is always part of

PEPPERONI

anchovies, aubergines, almonds, grapes, sausage

30. Complete the words which are synonyms, clockwise or anticlockwise.

31. What is the name given to a group of partridges? Is it:

   (a) caucus
   (b) clique
   (c) covey
   (d) covert
   (e) clamour

32. Which word means the same as

   VACILLATE

   hesitate, vanish, depose, improve, oscillate

33.

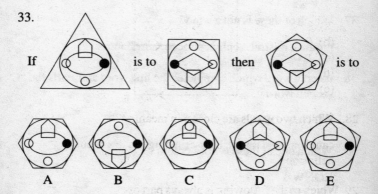

If ___ is to ___ then ___ is to

A   B   C   D   E

34. Solve the anagram (one word)

SEEN AS MIST

35. Which of these is the odd one out?

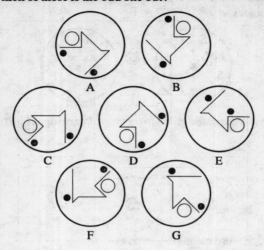

36. Which two words are opposite in meaning?

    trivial, renegade, coercion, loyalist, specious, celebrity

37. Which of these is not a wind?

    nimbus, mistral, zephyr, sirocco, hurricane

38. Insert a word which completes the first word and starts the second word

    HOT(. . . .)STONE

39. Which one of these is not a colour?

    RONWB
    WOYELL
    VUMAE
    CLECY
    SETRUS

40. Which of the following is the missing tile?

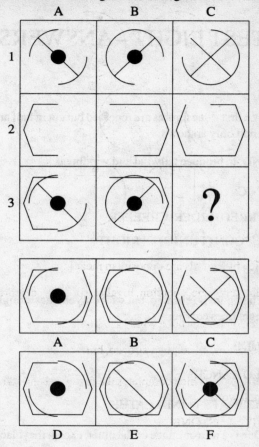

TEST EIGHT – ANSWERS

1. B. The first three figures are repeated but cut in half and the left-half only is shown.

2. WIND: to produce tailwind and windbreak.

3. TUNIC:

    STI²RRED³ ¹(RIDER)⁴ ²¹⁵³CREEPER⁵ ⁴
    SOUPCON² ³¹(TUNIC)⁴ ²¹⁵³UPRIGHT⁵ ⁴

4. angled

5. C. The figure is repeated, but with curved lines straight and straight lines curved.

6. CRUDE

7. ALLOWANCE

8. HIBERNATE or INBREATHE

9. B. One is a mirror image of the other, except that black and white are reversed.

10. ornament, decorate

11. useless

12. invade, inveighed

13. ponderous

14. B. The others are the same figure rotated.

15. B

16. mock, chaff

17. sprint: sprint is to run, the rest are to walk.

18. BAND to produce noseband and bandwagon.

19. IGABONE = BEGONIA. The fruits are satsuma, tangelo, avocado and pumpkin.

20. A. Large triangles are added to right and left in turn, firstly the right way up (one each side) then upside-down. All area covered by more than one triangle is shaded.

21. jigsaw

22. high

23. sack

24. (c) brownish colour

25. barouche: it is a horse-drawn carriage, the others are all boats.

26. (c) 8. In each segment the sum of the two outside numbers equals the opposite central number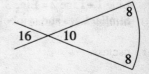

27. (c) 10

28. brasserie, restaurant

29. sausage

30. scampish, improper

31. (c) a covey

32. hesitate

33. A. The top and bottom symbols within the large circle
    switch round, as do the left and right symbols. The ellipse
    and the diamond shapes in the centre also switch. The large
    circle stays the same, and the outer shape adds an extra side.

34. steaminess

35. E.   A is the same as C + D.
           B is the same as F + G

36. renegade, loyalist

37. nimbus: a sort of cloud

38. head

39. CLECY = CYCLE. The colours are brown, yellow, mauve,
    russet.

40. C. Col A + Col. B = Col. C
    Line 1 + Line 2 = Line 3
    Similar lines and symbols disappear

TEST NINE

1.

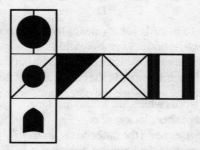

When the above is folded to form a cube, just one of the following can be produced. Which one?

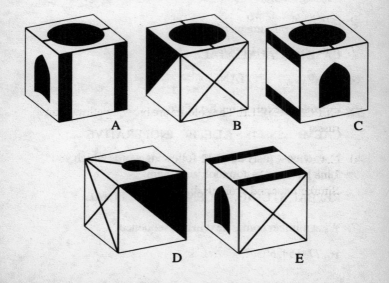

2.

Which option below continues the above sequence?

  A   B   C   D   E   F   G

3. Which word in the brackets means the same as the word in capitals?

   PALATIAL (empty, adequate, regal, luscious, important)

4. Find two words which are antonyms. One word reads either clockwise or anticlockwise round the outer circle and the other reads in the opposite direction in the inner circle. You must provide the missing letters.

5. Fill in the missing word:

   CASE (ESCALATE) TALE

   LEAP (. . . . .) TANS

6. Consider the following list of words:

   CALMNESS, FIRST, DEFER, INOPERATIVE

   Now choose just one of the following words which you think has most in common with them:

   REPEAT, STUDIO, ACCENT, PLACE, FINAL

7. What number comes next in this sequence?

   16, 77, 154, 605, ?

8. Which is the odd one out?

A   B   C   D   E

9. What word in the brackets is opposite in meaning to the word in capitals?

SUBDUE (ridicule, contest, commence, provoke, infer)

10. Which two words that sound alike but are spelled differently mean:

(a) yield
(b) limb

11. PREDILECTION is to LIKING as

PRESAGE is to omen, absurd, reputation, triumph, allege

12. What creature should go in the brackets reading downwards so as to convert the letters to the left of the brackets into three-letter words?

OA( )
SE( )
AL( )
TI( )
TO( )
RA( )

13. Underline the two words that are closest in meaning:

case, note, wall, wad, rock, lump

14.

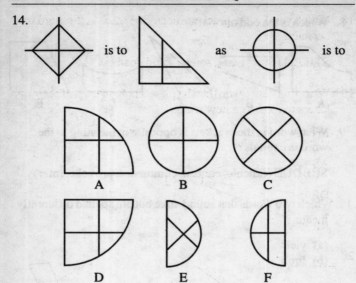

is to _____ as _____ is to

A   B   C

D   E   F

15. Which is the odd one out?

repeal, reduce, revoke, quash, abrogate

16. What word when placed in the bracket completes the first word and starts the second word?

WIN(. . . .)ONE

17. Which one of these is not a composer?

LIBZERO
LADIVVI
CINIPUC
SOAPSIC
DOORNIB

18. Which word in the brackets means the same as the word in capitals?

    STILL (kinetic, tense, serene, rigid, leaden)

19. What four-letter word can be placed behind each of these letters to form four new words?

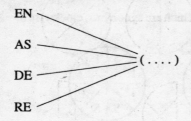

    EN
    AS
    DE   (. . . .)
    RE

20.

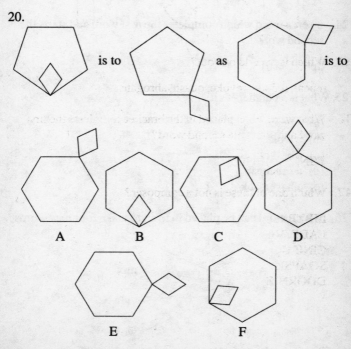

    is to   as   is to

    A   B   C   D

    E   F

21. Which is the odd one out?

apostate, mediator, benedict, freshman, portcullis

22. Solve the anagram (one word)

COD COILER

23. Complete the words which are synonyms, clockwise or anticlockwise

24. Insert a word which completes the first word and starts the second word

tip(. . .)nail

25. What is a pannier? Is it:

(a) a brace
(b) a wok
(c) a basket
(d) a saucepan
(e) a haversack

26. Which word can be placed in front to make four new words?

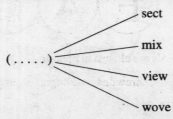

sect

mix

(. . . . .)

view

wove

27. Which domino is next in this sequence?

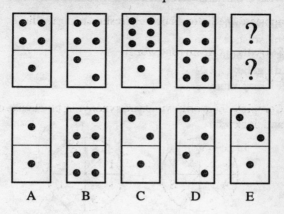

A   B   C   D   E

28. Which letter of the alphabet should appear in the blank circle?

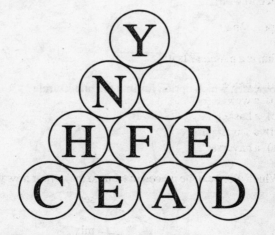

29. Which two words are closest in meaning?

impecuniousness, shrewdness, dotage, senility, portliness, triumphant

30. What is the name given to a group of stars? Is it:

    (a) penumbra
    (b) solstice
    (c) cosmology
    (d) galaxy
    (e) magnitude

31.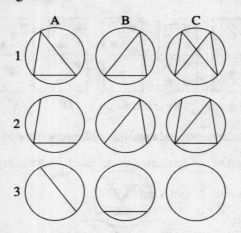

Logically, which option fits into the blank circle?

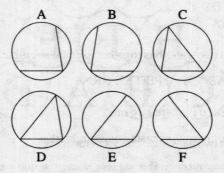

32. Which of the following is always part of

    BLANQUETTE

    marshmallow, apricots, veal, mutton, tripe

33. Insert the word that means the same as the definitions outside the brackets

    fish eggs (. . .) deer

34. Which word means the same as

    VACUOUS

    empty, stupid, full, varied, virtuous

35. Which two words are opposite in meaning?

    tiro, poltergeist, ambassador, matriarch, coward, expert

36. Which one of these is not food?

    BMAL
    ADREB
    TEBRUT
    TONCOT
    NOCBA

37. Place 3 two-letter bits together to equal an edible nut

    EL   AZ   SA   PE   KE   RN

38. Which of these is not a game?

    euchre, crambo, canasta, tombola, brisket

39.

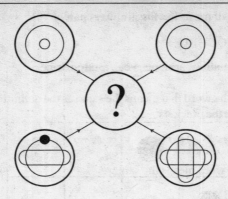

Each line and symbol which appears in the four outer circles, above, is transferred to the centre circle according to these rules:

If a line or symbol occurs in the outer circles:

   once: it is transferred
   twice: it is possibly transferred
   3 times: it is transferred
   4 times: it is not transferred.

Which of the circles shown below should appear at the centre of the diagram, above?

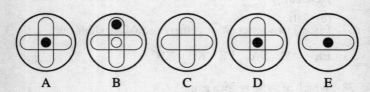

A   B   C   D   E

40. What is the value across the diagonal?

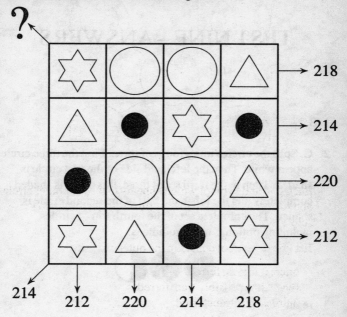

→ 218
→ 214
→ 220
→ 212

214
212 220 214 218

(a) 210
(b) 212
(c) 214
(d) 218
(e) 220

TEST NINE – ANSWERS

1. B.

2. C. Split the circles into groups of three. First the three circles
   appear white. Then the left hand side of the first circle is
   shaded. Then in the third set of three, this circle is shaded
   completely and the left-hand half of the second circle is
   shaded. The complete set of the fourth trio of circles,
   including option C in the middle is:

3. regal

4. contract, increase

5. PLEASANT. LEAP is an anagram of PLEA and TANS is an
   anagram of SANT. Similarly CASE is an anagram of ESCA
   and TALE is an anagram of LATE

6. STUDIO. All the words contain three consecutive letters of
   the alphabet: CA[LMN]ESS, FI[RST], [DEF]ER
   I[NOP]ERATIVE, [STU]DIO

7. 1111: reverse each number and add it to the original: 605 +
   506 = 1111

8. E. In all the others the shortest line is shown dotted.

9. provoke

10. bow/bough

11. omen

12. FALCON: to produce oaf, sea, all, tic, too and ran.

13. wad, lump

14. A. The cross (A) goes inside the top right hand quarter (B) of the original figure

15. reduce: means to lessen, the others mean to cancel completely.

16. SOME: to produce winsome and someone

17. SOAPSIC = PICASSO. He was an artist. The composers are Berlioz, Vivaldi, Puccini and Borodin

18. serene

19. SIGN: to produce ensign, assign, design and resign

20. C. The figure falls to the left on to its nearest base. The diamond flips into the hexagon.

21. portcullis: the rest are all people

22. crocodile

23. sagacity, wiseness

24. toe

25. (c) a basket

26. **INTER**: to make intersect, intermix, interview and interwove

27. C. There are two sequences:

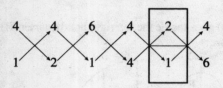

28. K. Change letters to numbers and add upwards:
    (A = 1, B = 2, C = 3 etc)

```
              25
         14       11 = K
      8       6       5
   3      5       1       4
```

29. dotage, senility

30. (d) galaxy

31. F. Col. A + Col. B = Col. C
    Line 1 + Line 2 = Line 3
    Similar lines disappear

32. veal

33. roe

34. empty

35. tiro, expert

36. TONCOT = COTTON. The others are lamb, bread, butter, bacon

37. kernel

38. brisket: it is a cut of meat

39. B.

40. (a) 210: ☆ = 51, ◯ = 55,

△ = 57, ● = 53

TEST TEN

1.

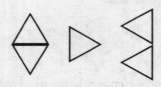

Which option below continues the above sequence?

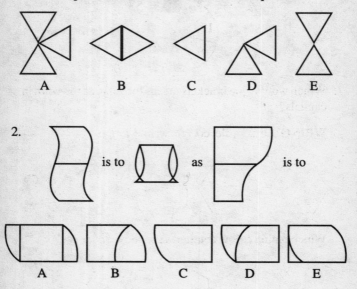

A   B   C   D   E

2. is to ... as ... is to

A   B   C   D   E

3. Which is the odd one out?

wallet, tap, realtor, postcode, paraffin

4. What word when placed in the brackets completes the first word and starts the second word?

   PORT(. . .)EAR

5. Which one of the these is not something you can wear?

   DROTALE
   WEARSET
   MYIHNCE
   RUFMOIN
   MYSHKAA

6. What number should replace the question mark?

7. Which word in the brackets means the same as the word in capitals?

   WRING (turn, girdle, coerce, writhe, dry)

8.

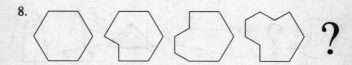

   Which option below continues the above sequence?

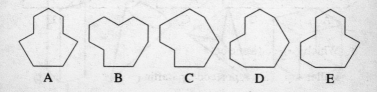

9. Underline the two words that are opposite in meaning:

   pernickety, friendly, hopeless, careless, pampered, personable

10. Which two words that sound alike but are spelled differently mean:

    (a) remainder
    (b) take by force

11. Insert the letters into the blanks to complete two words which mean the same as the words above them.

    AAAABEEIILRTTX

    OSTRACIZE   FIXABLE

    – – P – – R – – – E   – – P – – R – – – E

12. 456 is to 120 as

    789 is to 240, 450, 480, 504 or 702

13. Underline the two words that are closest in meaning:

    bevy, group, draught, bid, bout, efflux

14.

Which figure below should replace the question mark?

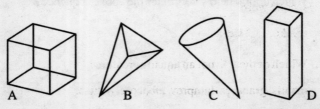

15. A number of synonyms of the keyword are shown. Take one letter from each of the synonyms to find a further synonym of the keyword. The letters appear in the correct order

    Keyword: ENDLESS

    Synonyms: CEASELESS, UNBOUNDED, ETERNAL, PERPETUAL, UNENDING, INCESSANT, UNLIMITED, CONSTANT, INTERMINABLE

16. What creature is missing from the brackets?

    a token (. . . .) close tightly

17. Consider the following list of words:

    FREIGHTER, BONESHAKER, DRIFTWOOD

    Now choose just one of the following words which you think has most in common with them.

    SAIL, CANINE, OCEAN, WRECKAGE, RENDER

18. Solve this nine-letter word anagram:

    I MADE TIME

19. What word in the brackets is opposite in meaning to the word in capitals?

    CAPACIOUS (inept, stable, poor, insecure, tiny)

20. Insert a word which completes the first word and starts the second word

    trunk(. . . .) side

21. Which of these is not an aquatic creature?

    mantis, grampus, lamprey, albacore, halibut

22.

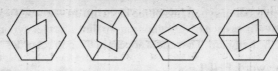

Which option below continues the above sequence?

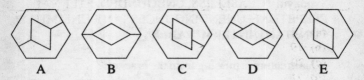

A   B   C   D   E

23. Complete the words which are synonyms clockwise or anticlockwise

24. What is the name given to a group of bears? Is it:

   (a) a sloth
   (b) a haggle
   (c) a pride
   (d) a stand
   (e) a murder

25. Which of the following is always part of a

NEGUS

shrimps, hot water, turnips, broccoli, semolina

26. Which is the odd one out?

tester, firkin, jacobus, scudo, kopeck

27. What is the total of the numbers on the reverse side of these dice?

   (a) 18
   (b) 19
   (c) 20
   (d) 21
   (e) 22

28. Which option fits into the blank circle to carry on a logical sequence?

A   B   C   D   E

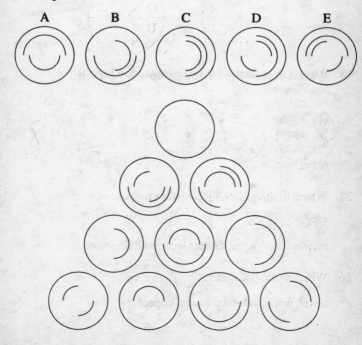

29. Which two words are closest in meaning?

    guardian, prisoner, itinerant, roving, teacher, pupil

30. Solve the anagram (one word)

    EMANATE

31. Place 3 two-letter bits together to mean 'of woods'

    LI   LV   SY   ME   TO   AN

32. Which word can be placed in
    front to make four new
    words?

    (. . . .)

    shelf
    binder
    mark
    maker

33. Which circle carries on the sequence to a logical
    conclusion?

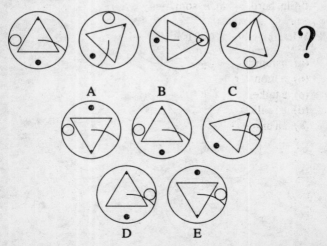

    A   B   C

    D   E

34. Which two words are opposite in meaning?

   debauchery, perverse, hackneyed, cheerlessness, purity, residential

35. Which of these is not an employed person?

   GENAT
   BIBAR
   VANVY
   RIVDRE
   NOCAB

36. Insert the word that means the same as the definitions outside the brackets

   pass (. .) Japanese game

37. Which word means the same as

   NUGATORY

   futile, herd, harsh, lissom, nutty

38. What is a jabberwok? Is it:

   (a) a utensil
   (b) a monster
   (c) a talker
   (d) a sealion
   (e) an arguer

39.

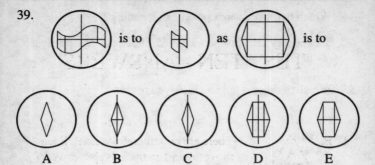

40.

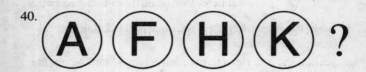

Which option below should logically follow in the above sequence?

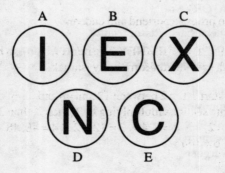

TEST TEN – ANSWERS

1. E. There are two triangle A and B. Each moves round on the axis shown by 45 degrees each time. Triangle A moves anticlockwise and triangle B clockwise.

2. B. The top half if folded down on to the bottom half.

3. realtor: the American term for an estate agent. The rest are English terms for which there is a different American term: wallet (billfold), tap (faucet), postcode (zip code) and paraffin(kerosene).

4. End: to produce portend and endear.

5. MYIHNCE = CHIMNEY. The items which can be worn are leotard, sweater, uniform and yashmak.

6. 1440: start at the 2 between 12 and 48 and jump clockwise to alternate sections multiplying by 1, then 2, then 3 etc:
   $2 \times 1 = 2, 2 \times 2 = 4, 4 \times 3 = 12, 12 \times 4 = 48, 48 \times 5 = 240,$
   $240 \times 6 = 1445$

7. coerce

8. E. One side in turn, working clockwise turns into an angle. Once a side has turned into an angle it points inwards then outwards in turn (always starting pointing inwards).

9. pernickety, careless

10. rest, wrest

11. expatriate, repairable

12. 504: $4 \times 5 \times 6 = 120$, $7 \times 8 \times 9 = 504$

13. bevy, group

14. C: the number of surfaces increase by one each time starting with a sphere (one surface). The cone (option C) has two surfaces

15. continual

16. seal

17. CANINE: it contains a number CA[NINE] as do FR[EIGHT]ER, B[ONE]SHAKER and DRIF[TWO]OD

18. immediate

19. tiny

20. road

21. mantis

22. C. The diamond rotates anticlockwise pointing at each corner (or pair of corners) in turn at each stage. The line rotates clockwise pointing at middle of line, corner, middle of line in turn.

23. ricochet, bouncing

24. (a) a sloth

25. hot water

26. firkin: it is a unit of measure, the rest are all names of currency

27. (c) 20: Number plus reverse always equals 7
so $6 + 2 + 3 + 4 + 5 = 20$

28. C. Each circle is obtained by combining the two lower circles. Similar parts of circles disappear

29. itinerant, roving

30. manatee: a sea cow

31. sylvan

32. book

33. A. △ moves 45 degrees clockwise
    ● moves 45 degrees clockwise
    ○ moves 90 degrees clockwise
    ＼ moves 90 degrees clockwise

34. debauchery, purity

35. NOCAB = BACON. The others are agent, rabbi, navvy, driver

36. go

37. futile

38. (b) a monster

39. B. The inner shape contracts into the vertical line on either side.

40. D. N: all the letters are made with 3 lines